Interactions in
Ecology and
Literature

Advanced Curriculum From Vanderbilt University's Programs for Talented Youth

Interactions in Ecology and Literature

Integrated Science and ELA Lessons for Gifted and Advanced Learners in Grades 2–3

Tamra Stambaugh, Ph.D.,
Eric Fecht, Ed.D.,
& Emily Mofield, Ed.D.

PRUFROCK PRESS INC.
WACO, TEXAS

Prufrock Press Inc.
P.O. Box 8813
Waco, TX 76714-8813
Phone: (800) 998-2208
Fax: (800) 240-0333
http://www.prufrock.com

Table of Contents

Acknowledgements

We would like to acknowledge Dr. Joyce VanTassel-Baska and her Integrated Curriculum Model that continues to inspire work in curriculum development and breathe life into content in ways that provide students with opportunities to access advanced content, explore content in depth and with complexity, and examine abstract relationships through concept development. We also acknowledge the content experts in various fields who willingly share their passions and expertise in ways that help us translate advanced content into student-centered lessons. Further, we acknowledge the teachers who piloted these units, provided honest feedback, and supported gifted students' talent development and expertise.

Introduction

Interactions in Ecology and Literature integrates the study of food webs and ecosystems with fictional and informational texts. This unit, developed by Vanderbilt University's Programs for Talented Youth, is aligned to the Common Core State Standards (CCSS) and Next Generation Science Standards (NGSS). In this unit students will examine relationships among living things and the environment as well as interactions between literary elements in texts and visuals through exposure to accelerated content, engaging activities, and differentiated tasks.

CONCEPTUAL FRAMEWORK

Interactions in Ecology and Literature is designed specifically for gifted elementary school students (grades 2–3) to support the acquisition of textual analysis skills, including identifying the relationship between literary elements within a text, enhancing thinking and communication skills, and connecting conceptual generalizations from crosscurricular themes through a variety of media, including literary texts, nonfiction texts, video, art, and guided explorations about ecology and interactions. The Integrated Curriculum Model (ICM; VanTassel-Baska, 1986) is the conceptual framework used for the unit design. Components of the framework are embedded in each lesson: accelerated content, advanced processes of the discipline (e.g., literary analysis, scientific inquiry), and conceptual understandings. For example, the accelerated content includes ELA standards, aligned to the CCSS. The CCSS selected for each unit are above the grade level(s) for which the unit was intended. Additionally, higher level resources are used in a variety of lessons. Each lesson also includes process skills and specific models or activities to help students analyze a variety of texts, art, and scientific phenomenon. The content of each lesson is connected by the overarching theme of interactions and key generalizations that span a variety of disciplines.

INTENDED GRADE LEVEL(S)

The positive academic effects of grouping gifted students and accelerating the content they are taught are well documented (see Assouline, Colangelo, VanTassel-Baska, & Lupkowski-Shoplik, 2015; Kulik & Kulik, 1992; Steenbergen-Hu, Makel, & Olszewski-Kubilius, 2016; Rogers, 2007). Not all elementary and middle schools, however, are designed to support accelerated courses for their high-achieving students. Experienced teachers of general classrooms may use this unit with their gifted and high-achieving students as part of a deliberate differentiated approach that includes in-class flexible groupings based on student needs.

This unit is intended for and has been piloted with gifted students in grades 2–3. The unit is aligned to CCSS and NGSS standards primarily focused on grades 4–5 with some lower grade standards included as needed. The accelerated content is necessary so that gifted students have the opportunity to gain new ELA content knowledge at a pace and level that is appropriate for their learning needs. Gifted students' readiness and experience levels vary, as do their abilities. Some gifted students may find this unit engaging as a second or third grader, while others may need to wait until grade 4 or 5 to fully participate and understand the unit concepts.

LESSON FORMAT AND GUIDELINES

Each lesson in this unit follows a similar format for ease of use. Teachers select from a variety of questions, activities, and differentiated products to best meet their students' needs. There are also opportunities for talent development and discussion of social-emotional components within the curriculum. Table 1 summarizes each lesson. Other key features of the unit and lessons are outlined in the following sections.

ALIGNMENT TO STANDARDS

The unit incorporates the key pedagogical shifts highlighted as part of the CCSS. For example, students read both literary and informational texts from a variety of sources and perspectives. Through the examination of multiple texts, they learn domain-specific content from their readings and are required to provide text-based evidence to support their answers or ideas. The ELA-focused lessons also support opportunities for students to make or analyze an argument, defend a position, or interpret a text. Of course, part of close reading and understanding of a text

Table 1
Lesson Summaries

	Lesson	Key Question	Summary
1	*Everything Interacts: Concept Introduction and* The Great Kapok Tree	How do the interactions of different textual elements help readers understand the purpose of a text?	Students are introduced to the concept of interactions and explore issues relating to deforestation using *The Great Kapok Tree* and a nonfiction pro/con text.
2	*Interactions Among Living and Nonliving Things: Ecosystems and Food Chains*	How do interactions between living and nonliving things impact the environment?	Students examine how living things interact through food chains and food webs. Following an exploration of the interactions between abiotic and biotic factors, environmental interactions for filling in a pond will be explored using the Science Analysis Wheel.
3	*Interactions and Literature: A Novel Study*	How does an author's use of character interactions develop the theme of the story?	While reading *The One and Only Ivan*, students examine literary components such as theme, symbolism, and characterization through a variety of activities that help them understand how an author uses character interactions to promote theme.
4	*Interactions and Perspective: Art Analysis*	How do different elements in a picture interact to create meaning?	Using *A Sunday Afternoon on the Island of La Grande Jatte* (1884) by Georges Seurat, students complete a visual analysis and examine the interactions between technique (pointillism), color, balance, etc., within art.
5	*Interactions and Balance: Simulating Ecosystems*	How do interactions among living things help support balance in ecosystems?	Students learn about the need for balance between living organism populations within an ecosystem. Using an online simulation, students begin to understand the need for larger populations of producers and smaller populations of consumers and that balance exists.
6	*Interactions Through Words and Images: Poetry Analysis*	What impact does the author's intentional interaction of words and images have on the meaning of a piece of literature or art?	Students analyze poems grounded in ecology and the concept of interactions. Students have opportunities to develop their own poems or artwork that include details about an animal's interactions within their environment.
7	*Interactions and Invasive Species: Overpopulation of Wild Boars*	What impact does an imbalance or an over-/underpopulation of one species have on an ecosystem?	Students learn about the impact that imbalance due to shifts in one organism population can have on an ecosystem. Exploring wild boar population growth, students complete a table and graphing exercise and examine ecological consequences and potential solutions.

Table 1, Continued.

	Lesson	Key Question	Summary
8	*Interactions Through Positive Relationships: Picture Book Study*	How can interactions help build positive relationships?	Using two picture books written by Jacqueline Woodson (*The Other Side* and *Each Kindness*), students learn about how interactions with others, through words and actions, can be used in positive or negative ways. Students explore the relationship between interactions among characters and plot.
9	*Interactions and Change: The True Story of Ivan*	Should animals be kept outside of their natural habitats?	After reading *Ivan: The Remarkable True Story of the Shopping Mall Gorilla*, students explore the issue of whether or not animals should be kept in zoos. Students compare the fictionalized version with the real-life account and create skits that emphasize their stance on the removal of animals from their natural habitats.
10	*Interactions and Teamwork*	How do group interactions help others survive?	Students explore ways in which animals work together to survive by examining specific species and how they interact in order to gather food, protect themselves, communicate, migrate, or adjust to changes in their environment. Students apply newly learned information about interactions between and among species to the characters they have read about throughout the unit.
11	*Interactions Within Us: Biography Study*	How do a person's interactions with his or her life experiences impact his or her future?	Using songs from animated films and biographies of J. K. Rowling, Michael Jordan, and Walt Disney, students explore how individuals interact with their own life experiences, especially failure, and ways in which those interactions impact their future.
12	*Culminating Project*	What role do interactions play in ecosystems and literature?	Students are provided various options to demonstrate their understanding of content and concept connections throughout the unit through a project of their choice.

includes the use of domain-specific vocabulary. The readings selected throughout the unit build upon specific concepts and highlight multiple perspectives. Many readings use vocabulary of the specific discipline or advanced concepts, which students must understand and attempt to define. Science lessons also incorporate the NGSS in grades 3–5.

The beginning of each lesson includes a list of the overarching goals and objectives as well as CCSS or NGSS specific to each lesson. The end of the unit includes a CCSS alignment chart and an NGSS chart. This unit was not designed to meet every CCSS ELA or NGSS standard for a particular grade level but focuses in depth on advanced skills and accelerated content. Supplemental information may be necessary to complement a full literature or science course and ensure that all required content for a specific grade level is taught.

Materials

When differentiating for the gifted, it is important for the materials and readings to be at a level commensurate with the student's ability. The readings and resources in this unit have been carefully selected and include either sophisticated concepts or reading selections at or above the indicated grade levels. The materials section includes a list of resources needed for the lesson. Some of the listed materials are optional, and many of the selected texts, visuals, or videos are readily available online as a free download. When possible, reliable sites and specific links, available at the time of this unit's printing, are provided. *A word of caution*: It is important to note that some of the readings or some concepts may be controversial or contain advanced or sensitive concepts and content. It is up to the teacher and school administration to understand the context of his or her district and to determine whether or not a reading or scientific discussion is appropriate or whether a different text or discussion-based question should be used.

Introductory Activities

The introductory activities provide a real-world connection or "hook" that sets the tone for the remainder of the lesson and enhances student engagement. Sample options include quick debates about an issue or dilemma, illustrations to convey a key concept or idea, or key discussion questions that help students better understand the relevance of a lesson's text, art, or science concepts. Often these introductory debate topics or discussion questions are revisited at the close of the lesson, allowing students to revisit and review their initial answer or stances given newly absorbed content.

In-Class Activities to Deepen Learning

The activities included here provide hands-on or thought-provoking ideas that support or solidify student learning. Tasks incorporate hands-on activities, real-world connections, and opportunities to construct scientific explanations through the development and use of models. They may include issue-based questions linked to a big idea, quick debates, scientific investigations, or technology extensions. These activities also include opportunities for self-reflection on how the lesson content impacted their learning. The activities in this section are intended to be taught as part of the main lesson.

Choice-Based Differentiated Products

Several choice-based differentiated products are also part of each lesson. Students may select one of the choice products to showcase their strengths and individual understanding of a particular content area or, if pressed for time, teachers may require two or three choice-based products for students to complete during the course of the unit. The options listed allow students an opportunity to pursue their interests and to gain a deeper understanding of a learning objective as they present their understanding in a creative way. Differentiated products vary by lesson and may include investigating a real-world problem, designing visuals to represent abstract ideas or conceptual understanding, applying an advanced model to other related sources, writing essays, and developing products or presentations for an audience. Rubrics are provided in Appendix C to guide product creation and teacher feedback. The rubrics may also be used for peer and self-evaluations.

Opportunities for Talent Development

Students need opportunities to build upon their interests, strengths, and curiosity in ways that expose them to new ideas and allow for them to extend their learning. This section provides students with ideas and opportunities to extend their learning in a variety of ways connected to the lesson, including career exposure.

Social-Emotional Connections

Social-emotional connections are an important part of processing and understanding oneself in addition to relating to events in a story or scientific phenomenon. The social-emotional connections are meant to encourage students to identify with story characters, biographies, and lives of scientists; reflect upon their personal stories; and consider life paths and careers and what a scientist or author does.

ELA Tasks

Designed with the CCSS assessments in mind, the ELA tasks support the writing and argument analysis items typically assessed as part of a state assessment. The ELA tasks incorporate multiple standards and require complex thinking. Students are asked to respond to a prompt by creating an essay in which they create or analyze arguments, critique texts, explain an issue from multiple perspectives, or explain the development of key concepts presented in an informational or fictional text. It is at the teacher's discretion to determine how many practice tasks students should write throughout the course of the unit. Although not explicitly stated in the unit, teachers are encouraged to model the writing and literary analysis process, help students analyze exemplars and inappropriate responses, and provide individual feedback.

Concept Connections

The concept connections section focuses on the third component of the ICM. The purpose of this section is to help students see the relationships between different texts and perspectives as these relate to key generalizations about interactions. A graphic organizer comprised of the conceptual generalizations and key unit readings is provided in the unit to help students organize their ideas and determine connections among the various readings and scientific investigations. It is important to refer to the concept generalizations in each lesson, even if the concept chart is not completed for every lesson. It is also recommended that teachers create a working wall that students can continue to build upon throughout the unit. Teachers may post the specific concept generalizations on a wall or bulletin board and ask students to add relevant content understanding and connections between concepts and content to the wall after each lesson. This can be used as an informal assessment and way to help students continue to reflect upon and process their learning.

Assessment

The assessment section focuses on assessing a student's understanding of a single-faceted objective, such as analyzing a previously conducted inquiry-based science activity, making inferences, or determining how an author used a literary element to convey an idea or theme. The assessments may be used to determine the extent to which students understand the meaning of a text or scientific content and can provide supporting evidence and target instruction based on individual needs. Teachers may require students to complete an assessment, a variety of different formative assessment tasks throughout the lesson (e.g., responses to questions, concept connections), or differentiated product tasks so that students' thinking and understanding can be measured in a variety of ways. Additionally, exit tickets are included in this section to check for understanding of various lesson concepts and content. They may be used to guide whether or not teachers need to reteach portions of a lesson or concept.

Handouts

Following each lesson, all necessary handouts for lesson completion are included (e.g., readings, visuals, organizers, blank analysis models, inquiry-based science guides, and other sources not readily available online). As previously stated in the materials section, sometimes teachers are led to specific web-based links or it is recommended that popular sources be found online. This is especially important for featured art or graphs (which may not copy well). Also know that if picture books are recommended, teachers may be able to find read alouds in their classroom, school library, or online through general web-based searches.

Other Unit Features

This unit includes a culminating lesson that synthesizes many of the learning objectives into a comprehensive project so that students may showcase their learning in a creative way. These options may include the application of the advanced content learned throughout the unit, real-world problem solving, and the development of authentic products. Additionally, the culminating lesson includes opportunities for students to focus on in-depth self-reflections that relate concept-themes to real-world connections. Rubrics are provided so that students understand the expectations of a task and teachers can easily analyze student products given set criteria. The rubrics are also useful for peer and self-evaluations.

Teacher background information is another feature found in some lessons. Although some background information is provided, teachers are encouraged to study specific literary analysis critiques for a particular reading, and seek varied interpretations of the text or visual. When needed, lessons include a section on background knowledge, primarily as videos teachers can watch or links to suggested articles. We encourage teachers to view this information well in advance of lesson implementation.

Sample responses are also included for some of the more complex questions and analysis models. It is important to understand that the answers provided are a guide and should not be construed as the only correct response. Student answers will vary, and many unanticipated responses may be correct. Teachers are encouraged to use the provided answers to better understand the intent of the question, to model how to arrive at an appropriate response, to demonstrate how to use a specific analysis model, and to familiarize themselves with the intent of a particular passage.

Finally, this unit features instructions for using models, sample lessons, blank model handouts, and guides to support students' thinking about each element of a given analysis model. Rubrics are also provided to assess student products and responses. Specifically, Appendix A highlights instructions, handouts, and examples for each analysis model. Appendix B includes blank models and guides for thinking about each element of a particular model, and Appendix C includes rubrics for assessing student progress.

Time Allotment

Most lessons can be taught within 90–120 minutes, although some lessons may take longer. The length of the lesson also depends upon how many models and activities are employed, how interested students are in a particular issue or text, the length of the text, and time needed for fully experimenting and understanding inquiry-based science lessons. The length may also depend on how many times a text needs to be read or analyzed or a science lesson needs to be discussed or retaught for students to gain understanding. In general, it is anticipated that this unit can be taught with approximately 20–25 hours of instructional time if teachers follow the recommended guidelines as reported in this section.

Differentiation

Gifted students are a heterogeneous group and their ability levels, pace of learning, interests, and depth of understanding vary. Although this unit was written with gifted elementary school students in mind, differentiation is still necessary. A variety of differentiated opportunities are embedded in the unit, such as choice-based product options, open-ended questions, and more simple and complex ways to adapt the analysis models and adjust instruction based on students' readiness and interest levels.

In addition to the individual lesson activities and differentiated product options found in each lesson, the final lesson synthesizes unit goals and provides opportunities for students to select a project of their own choosing to explore in depth. The close reading questions can also be differentiated. Teachers may assign specific questions or tasks to individual students or groups of students based on their responses from formative assessments, concept maps, science lessons, or ELA tasks.

The ELA process model (e.g., literary analysis) is easily differentiated as well. For example, the literary wheels and cubes automatically provide a framework for teachers to ask simple questions using only one element, or more complex questions by emphasizing relationships among various elements (e.g., how setting influences conflict, how figurative language contributes to characterization). Examples of simple and complex questions are included in selected lessons and also in Appendix A. The teacher may also differentiate the in-class activities by assigning different groups of students to specific tasks. These can be designed as differentiated stations for science and ELA lessons. Of course, not all students would complete work at every station but would be assigned a station based on their readiness. After the complexity of the task is established, activities, questions, or product choices are then incorporated to accommodate various learning needs. The process is similar for science and the use of the Science Analysis Wheel, Text Analysis Wheel, and the Visual Analysis Wheel (also in Appendix A).

Assessment and Grading

Formative, diagnostic-prescriptive, and summative performance-based assessments are an essential part of the unit. Assessment data come from a variety of sources and are used to monitor student growth, provide student feedback, allow for student self-reflection, or to differentiate content or instruction. Descriptions of the assessments used in this unit are as follows:

- **Diagnostic-prescriptive assessment:** The unit pretest provides a first glimpse of a student's current level of performance. Each question focuses on a different key understanding. For example, Question 1 focuses on the relationship between different literary elements, Question 2 focuses on making inferences and providing evidence, and Question 3 focuses on concepts or themes. To assess student learning on science objectives, Question 4 focuses on the scope and depth of a student's understanding of science content related to ecological interactions. Responses for each question can be used to differentiate questions for different groups of students and to assign specific tasks that support student learning in a key area. Prior to Lesson 1, administer the pretest and use the rubric to score responses, and use this data and other information gathered throughout the unit for ongoing differentiation.

- **Formative assessment:** There are many opportunities throughout the unit for teachers to check for student understanding. Teachers may occasionally ask students to expand, in writing, upon their answer to an assigned question from the text-dependent questions or their understanding of scientific phenomena being studied to assess textual understanding or science content. The assessment section activities may also be assigned and graded to determine the level of student understanding as well as misconceptions about specific sources or texts that may need reteaching or further exploration. It is not recommended that every lesson's assessment task be assigned or graded, although teachers may select two or three of each throughout the course of the unit to use for this purpose. Informally, teachers may gather formative assessment data by listening to student discussions to ensure that students are learning the information presented and mastering or exceeding the goals. Differentiated choice products may also be used as a formative assessment and graded using the provided rubric. Exit tickets can also be used as a quick check for understanding. Teachers should encourage students to engage in self-reflection as they receive feedback from a variety of assessments. Additionally, it is recommended that students continue to build and develop a concept map-working wall for the concept of interactions as well as the scientific content being learned. It may be helpful to create a concept map-working wall that lists specific generalizations for interactions as outlined in this unit. Students can add specific content-based examples that fit under each concept for ELA and for science, using two different colors. Students may also continue to build upon their own science-only content map to show their understanding of interactions in ecosystems.

- **Summative assessment:** There are two different summative assessments in the unit. The final lesson (Lesson 12) includes culminating choice-based products for students to showcase their understanding of key unit content, processes, and concepts through selected product-creations. In addition, the postassessment of the unit can be used as a summative assessment and also to measure student growth, when compared with the preassessment.

MAKING THE MOST OUT OF THE UNIT

The following ideas are important to consider before teaching the unit:
- Provide professional development about the units that includes both content and pedagogy. Some of the unit content is complex, and background knowledge may be needed. Read Appendix A instructions and examples for using the analysis models before teaching the unit. Practice completing the models on your own using specific texts before asking the students to do so until you are familiar with the models.
- For those students who need more scaffolding in ELA or science, consider teaching the models, expectations, and processes separately first with easier texts to get students accustomed to different ways of thinking before adding complex resources, issues, and concepts.
- You may need to teach the individual elements of each analysis model before combining them. Still, it isn't necessary to teach an entire unit on characterization or setting, for example, before using the literary analysis model, although students may need explanations and practice applying the

individual elements first if they haven't been exposed to those ideas prior to this unit. This can be done in context and not separately. Because gifted students learn at a faster pace, teaching individual elements can be done more quickly so that you can focus on depth and complexity through the relationships between the different elements.

- Read the texts and prompts ahead of time to make sure the selections are appropriate for your district context. Substitute readings and visuals as appropriate. Similarly, in science, read the background knowledge information or follow the URLs provided to learn more, prior to teaching the lesson—especially if the content is unfamiliar. Attempt the inquiry-based assignments prior to teaching each science lesson, so that you can predict potential outcomes of the simulations or experiments, better support student learning, and provide tips or predict potential issues students may encounter. For both ELA and science lessons, make sure the online resources and videos are still available before teaching a particular lesson. All URLs were active at the time of this printing.

- Follow your students. Sometimes a lesson or reading may prompt important discussions that continue beyond the allotted time period.

- Know the intent of the models and the lesson outcomes so that you can best guide students toward important process, content, and concept goals. Otherwise, the issues discussed may supersede the objectives, especially with passionate gifted students. Don't assign text-dependent questions as in-depth writing activities or homework as the norm. Discussion and teacher feedback are important, and most of the questions in the unit are intended to be part of a small- or whole-group discussion. By engaging students through group discussions, you can correct misconceptions right away and solicit multiple perspectives and ideas that can enhance student learning. Similarly, know that differentiated tasks and talent development sections are not intended to be assigned for every lesson or as homework for each student. Instead these opportunities for talent development and assignment tasks are options that may be used in some lessons to further extend student learning. Teachers may require that students complete at least two differentiated tasks or talent development assignments for the entire unit.

- Be sure to emphasize the use of supporting evidence and the complex relationships among various elements of a model when facilitating student discussions.

- Have fun! We hope these units not only show academic gains in your students similar to what we have observed but also encourage them to become citizens who can critically analyze situations and enact positive change.

UNIT GENERALIZATIONS

- Interactions are inevitable.
- Interactions allow for changes.
- Interactions are caused by multiple influences.
- Interactions can be positive, negative, or mutually beneficial.

UNIT GOALS AND OBJECTIVES

Content

English language arts: To analyze and interpret fiction, nonfiction, and art, students will be able to:
- analyze how literary elements interact to promote meaning within a story or poem;
- cite evidence in discussion and writing to support a point of view illuminated through literature, art, or nonfiction; and
- evaluate how an author uses language, structure, and point of view to reveal purpose and/or advance a claim.

Science: To understand ecosystems, students will be able to:
- synthesize information to explain how interactions in an environment among living things bring about change;
- analyze the relationship among living organisms in an environment;
- analyze how scientific elements (energy, structure, patterns, findings, etc.) interact to explain or solve an issue or problem;
- cite examples of food chains from different environments;
- demonstrate the flow of energy within a food chain;
- explain the relationship between producers, consumers, and decomposers and the sun;
- explain the relationships and provide examples of interactions between living and nonliving things;
- discuss reasons why animals live in groups;
- analyze the relationship between population growth in one species and the impact on other living things; and
- explain and demonstrate how natural and manmade changes in ecosystems lead to positive or negative changes for living organisms.

Process

English language arts: To develop interpretation, analysis, and communication skills in the language arts, students will be able to:

- respond to an analysis of literature, nonfiction, or art by developing arguments or elaborating on explanations through writing a variety of texts (e.g., essays and paragraphs, including relevant and sufficient evidence to support claims); and
- use evidence to develop inferences, justify arguments, and develop claims.

Science: To apply knowledge of ecosystems, students will be able to:

- use food web models to analyze the flow of energy and the interactions among living organisms within an ecosystem;
- create models to explain what happens to a food web when abiotic and biotic factors change;
- design models that show scientific understanding of different content;
- create a model using a computer simulation to evaluate the flow of energy and interactions among living organisms within a food web;
- use evidence to develop conclusions about the flow of energy and the need for balance among organism populations;
- create and interpret graphs related to population growth of living organisms;
- analyze data related to the population growth of one species and its impact on the population of another species;
- compare and contrast how animals behave before and after changes within their ecosystems or habitats; and
- debate the implications and consequences of keeping animals in captivity.

Concept

To develop conceptual thinking about interactions in language arts and science, students will be able to:

- explain how interactions promote change in multiple contexts across multiple disciplines;
- synthesize information from various texts, sources, and models to support generalizations about interactions;
- use inductive reasoning to develop generalizations about interactions;
- examine the relationship between interactions, relationships, and change in multiple contexts; and
- explain how interactions promote stability and change within an environment.

Pretest
"The Ant and the Grasshopper" *by Aesop*

PART I

Directions: Read the passage and respond to the following questions, citing evidence from the text. Complete the questions within 15 minutes, using a separate sheet of paper if necessary.

> The Ants were feasting on wheat that had been collected in the summertime. A Grasshopper, starving to death, came upon the ants and begged for a little food. The Ants inquired, "Why did you not gather and store your own food during the summer?" He replied, "I did not have enough time. I passed the days in singing." Together they said, "If you were foolish enough to sing all the summer, you cannot dance in the winter." It is important to work hard and plan for the future.
> —"The Ant and the Grasshopper" by Aesop

1. Explain how the different elements of the story (e.g., use of words, point of view, setting, characters, ideas, plot/conflict, images/symbols, etc.) help us understand the moral of the story.

2. In your own words, explain what the grasshopper meant when he said, "I did not have enough time. I passed the days in singing."

Pretest, Continued

3. How is what you know about interactions evident in the story? Use specific examples to support your ideas.

PART II

Directions: Develop a concept map about what you know about ecosystems on a separate sheet of paper.

4. Write *ecosystems* in the center, and draw spokes to other ideas related to ecology. You can add more connections to the new ideas you add.

   As you create a concept map, list all of the words you may know about the topic as separate boxes. The following words may be helpful. You do not need to use all of these words, and you may use other words you know as well: *environment, plants, animals, predators, prey, interactions, food chain, food web, pollination, habitat, change, energy, decomposer, omnivore, herbivore, carnivore, grow, live, die, adaptation,* etc.

   Make sure you show how the words you chose are related. Don't just write the words *habitat* and *change*, for example, as two different boxes on your map. Instead show connections by drawing lines between different words. Label the connections between the words you write. For example, you could draw a line to connect the words *habitat* and *change*, and then write a word that shows how they are related. Connect as many ideas together as you can.

Pretest Rubric
"The Ant and the Grasshopper" *by Aesop*

	0	1	2	3	4
Question 1: Content: Literary Analysis	Provides no response.	Response is limited and vague. There is no connection to how literary elements contribute to the meaning or moral. A literary element is merely named.	Response is accurate with 1–2 literary techniques described with vague or no connection to a moral. Response includes limited or no evidence from text.	Response is appropriate and accurate, describing at least two literary elements and a moral. Response is literal and includes some evidence from the text.	Response is insightful and well-supported, describing at least two literary elements and how they enhance the moral. Response includes abstract connections and adequate evidence from the text.
Question 2: Process: Inference From Evidence	Provides no response.	Response is limited, vague, and/or inaccurate. The explanation or inference is not valid.	Response is accurate, but lacks adequate explanation. Response includes a weak inference.	Response is accurate and makes sense. Response includes a valid inference.	Response is accurate and well-written. Response includes a thoughtful and valid inference.
Question 3: Concept/Theme Applied to Literature	Provides no response.	Response is limited, vague, and/or inaccurate.	Response lacks adequate explanation. Response does not relate or create a generalization about interactions. Little or no evidence from text.	Response is accurate and makes sense. Response relates to or creates an idea about interactions with some relation to the text.	Response is accurate, insightful, and well-written. Response relates to or creates a generalization about interactions with evidence from the text.
Question 4: Content: Science	Provides no response.	Provides a limited number of examples of ecosystems or provides multiple examples that include inaccurate or irrelevant information.	Provides multiple and accurate examples but does not show relationships (or shows inaccurate relationships) among or between the examples listed.	Provides multiple examples and includes at least four accurate relationships among or between the examples provided.	Provides multiple examples and includes advanced and content-specific vocabulary with five or more accurate relationships among or between the examples provided.

Note: Adapted with permission from Stambaugh & VanTassel-Baska, 2011, and Center for Gifted Education, 2010.

Interactions in Ecology and Literature © Prufrock Press Inc.

Lesson

Everything Interacts: Concept Introduction and *The Great Kapok Tree*

Key Question

How do the interactions of different textual elements help readers understand the purpose of a text?

Objectives

Content: To analyze and interpret fiction, nonfiction, and art, students will be able to:

- analyze how literary elements interact to promote meaning within a story or poem; and
- evaluate how an author uses language, structure, and point of view to reveal purpose and/or advance a claim.

To understand ecosystems, students will be able to:

- synthesize information to explain how interactions in an environment among living things bring about change; and
- analyze the relationship between living organisms in an environment.

Process: To develop interpretation, analysis, and communication skills in the language arts, students will be able to:

- respond to an analysis of literature, nonfiction, or art by developing arguments or elaborating on explanations through writing a variety of texts (e.g., essays and paragraphs, including relevant and sufficient evidence to support claims).

Concept: To develop conceptual thinking about interactions in the language arts and science, students will be able to:

- use inductive reasoning to develop generalizations about interactions; and
- examine the relationship between interactions generalizations in multiple contexts.

Accelerated CCSS for ELA

- RL.4.1
- RL.4.2
- RL.4.3
- RL.4.7

- RI.4.2
- RI.4.6
- W.4.2d
- W.4.9

- SL.5.1c
- SL.5.1d
- L.4.6

Accelerated NGSS

- 3-LS4-4

Materials

- *The Great Kapok Tree: A Tale of the Amazon Rain Forest* by Lynne Cherry (to read aloud; one copy for each small group—optional)
- Chart paper and markers (for small groups of students)
- Sticky notes (one medium-sized pack per student; or a stack of blank sticky note-sized scrap paper or small note cards)
- Handout 1.1: Literary Analysis Cubes (optional; folded into cubes)
- Handout 1.2: Blank Literary Analysis Wheel—Primary (if not using cubes)
- Handout 1.3: Deforestation Pros and Cons
- Handout 1.4: Blank Text Analysis Wheel—Primary
- Handout 1.5: Concept Organizer
- Rubric 1: Product Rubric (Appendix C)

Introductory Activities

1. Explain to students that they will be learning about interactions among animals, people, books, art, words, and the environment. Ask: *What is an interaction?* Solicit a variety of responses. Explain that "inter-" means *between*. So "inter-" actions are actions between different living and nonliving things.
2. Give each student a set of sticky notes or scrap paper. Ask students to walk around the room and look outside, noticing different people, animals, insects, plants, and objects that interact. Have them record each interaction on a separate note.
3. Divide students into pairs or small groups. Ask them to combine their interaction examples with their partner(s) and organize them into different categories.
4. Afterward, discuss:
   - What is similar about all of the interactions we shared?
   - What are the differences?

- What are some different reasons why things interact? (Sample response: To help each other, serve a common goal, survive, get food, communicate, etc.)
- Can nonliving things interact? (Sample response: Living things can interact with living and nonliving things.)
- What are some positive interactions you noticed? Negative interactions? Neutral interactions? Explain.
- What might happen in our environment or classroom if interactions did not occur?
- Can someone live without interacting?

5. Explain: *In this unit, we will be focusing on four generalizations about interactions (a generalization is a statement that is true across multiple objects, situations, subject areas, and things):*
   - Interactions are inevitable.
   - Interactions allow for changes.
   - Interactions are caused by multiple influences.
   - Interactions can be positive, negative, or mutually beneficial.

6. Display these generalizations in the classroom, as these will be referred to throughout the unit. You may also consider creating a concept map-working wall so students can add their connections between the content and concepts they learn each lesson.

7. Distribute chart paper to each group. Assign each group a different generalization. Tell groups to write their generalization in the middle of the chart paper and then create a concept map that shows at least five different examples that represent their generalization in another subject area or in their lives. Afterward, conduct a gallery walk for students to view and ask questions about each other's generalization posters.

In-Class Activities to Deepen Learning

1. **Engage students in a quick debate:** *Should humans cut down trees for purposes of shelter or safety?* Students can stand on opposite sides of the room to defend their point of view. Solicit a variety of responses.
2. Divide students into small groups. Distribute a copy of *The Great Kapok Tree* to each group. Have students explore the cover of the book, paying attention to the interactions that they see. (These may be the interaction of colors, animals and nature, words and pictures, etc.) Ask them to discuss which generalizations about interactions are noticeable from the cover.

3. Tell students that as you read you want them to pay attention to interactions found within the text. Read aloud *The Great Kapok Tree*, or conduct a reader's theater by assigning different students to read an animal part. The narrator reads all of the parts that are not spoken by the animals.

4. After reading, ask the following text-dependent questions:

   ▪ What interactions were important to the story (i.e., man and the tree, man and the animals, the animals with each other, man and his environment)? How did these interactions bring about change?

   ▪ The boa constrictor initially tells the sleeping man, "This is a tree of miracles . . . " Explain what this statement means.

   ▪ What benefit does the tree provide each animal? What benefits do the animals provide the tree? How are the interactions mutually beneficial? What examples from the story tell you this?

   ▪ Who or what do you think is the most central character in this story—the man, the animals, or the tree? Why?

   ▪ What is the main conflict or problem in the story, and what is done to resolve it?

   ▪ How does the author use the illustrations to help the reader understand the impact of the man cutting down the tree? (There is an increase in the number of animals who live in or depend upon the tree gathering together as the story progresses.)

   ▪ What does the great kapok tree symbolize (e.g., hope, life, survival, preservation)? (If students are unfamiliar with symbols, help them recognize that a symbol is something that represents something else. They may understand that a heart may symbolize love, a flag may symbolize freedom, a flower may symbolize life, dark clouds might symbolize sadness or gloom.)

   ▪ How does this story make you feel? Why? (Explain that "mood" is the reader's feeling when reading a story.) What then is the mood of the story? How does the author accomplish that through illustrations and words? Does the mood change or remain the same throughout the story? Explain.

   ▪ How do the illustrations of the man change throughout the course of the story? Notice his facial features and how the illustrator positions the man on each page. Why is this important to the meaning? (As the illustrations progress, the focus is on the man, with his image becoming increasingly larger or close up, as the story becomes all about whether or not he will destroy the animals' home. Although his eyes are initially shut, they open, as he has been enlightened by the information shared by the animals.)

- The bee tells the sleeping man, "You see, all living things depend on one another." What is the bee saying about interactions? What other interaction examples are present in the story?
- What is the author's message about natural resources? Changes in the environment? Changes in people?

Literary Analysis Questions With Added Complexity

1. Divide students into small groups based on their understanding of the story and readiness levels.
2. Provide each small group with two Literary Analysis Cubes (Handout 1.1) or the Literary Analysis Wheel—Primary (Handout 1.2). Tell students that not only do characters interact with each other or other things (i.e., nature) in a story, but authors also use interactions of different story elements and techniques to convey a message.
3. Explain that students will be examining different ways in which different story elements interact by either rolling cubes or using the Literary Analysis Wheel—Primary and drawing arrows to show interactions. Guide students through the following questions using the wheel or the cubes. If this is the first time using the wheel or the cubes, you may need to explain some of the categories. Additional information and examples can be found in Appendix A.
   - **Setting + Characters:** How does the setting of the rainforest, and more specifically the Great Kapok Tree, influence how the characters respond to the man? Provide examples from the story.
   - **Use of Words/Techniques + Characters:** How does the author help us understand the importance of the Great Kapok Tree as being vital to life? (Sample response: The number of animals that live in the tree help us understand the tree's importance for a variety of animals.)
   - **Sequence/Plot + Characters:** How does the introduction of each animal add to the conflict of the story?
   - **Feelings of Author (Tone) and Reader (Mood) + Setting:** How does the setting of the animals in *The Great Kapok Tree* contribute to the feelings you have as a reader?
   - **Use of Words/Techniques + Theme:** Onomatopoeia is a literary form that uses a word to mimic the sound of what it is describing. For example, the word *splash* sounds like a splash; the word *buzz* sounds like the buzzing of a bee. How does the author use onomatopoeia to help the reader understand the interactions of the story?
   - **Characters + Point of View:** How does the author use different close-up and far-away photos of the man to help us understand how he changes over time?

- **Point of View + Sequence/Plot:** How does the point of view and order of different animals introduced in the story add to the conflict? (Sample response: The arguments of the animals and what they contribute because of the tree's shelter are used to convince the man of what he should do, providing a cumulative effect.)
- **Structure and Style + Theme:** Look at the specific number of animals represented on each page. How does the author use the number of animals that continue to increase throughout the story to convey the importance of conserving the kapok tree?

4. Assign each group one of the following animals from the story: bee, monkeys, birds (toucan, macaw, cock of the rock), jaguar, porcupines, anteaters, or sloths. Ask students to reread the message their assigned animal relays to the man and discuss the following questions: *What is the effect of cutting down the tree, as their assigned animal reports it? What are the long-term or future issues that would occur if their animal left or died (implications)?* Create a chart to record student responses after they have had time to discuss the effects and implications. Table 2 provides some example responses.

5. Tell students you are going to revisit the question, "Should humans cut down trees?" by reading about reasons for and against deforestation (cutting down trees). Divide students into two groups. Distribute a copy of Handout 1.3: Deforestation Pros and Cons to each student. Ask students to read the entire article. Discuss as follows:
   - What are the benefits of deforestation?
   - What are the problems with deforestation?
   - Which argument do you think is stronger, the pro or the con? Why?

6. After their initial reading, introduce students to Handout 1.4: Text Analysis Wheel—Primary. As this may be the first time students have interacted with the Text Analysis Wheel—Primary, model the process for completing individual elements in the wheel before making connections. Ask the following questions and encourage students to jot down key words on their individual wheel as you discuss each section:
   - What is the main idea of the text you read?
   - What are the key ideas about deforestation?
   - What points of view are discussed? What other points of view should be considered?
   - What are the positive or negative implications of deforestation over time?

Table 2
Cause, Effect, and Implications Sample Responses

Cause: Man Cuts Down the Tree	
Effect	**Implications Over Time**
Bees will have fewer flowers to pollinate	Fewer flowers means the decline of plants or rainforest growth; no more food for some animals who need plants
Erosion; tree cannot stop water	Flooding; changes in the environment to a desert or dirt from washing away (monkeys say this)
Jaguar won't have any animals to eat	Animal populations may grow out of control; there will be too many animals competing for the same food, and they will either die or eat too many plants or other animals; everything will eventually die off

- How is the article structured? In what ways does this help you know what it will be about?
- Is this article fact or opinion? How do you know?

7. Next, explain that interactions occur between different textual elements as well. Guide students through the following questions, drawing arrows or guiding students to think about the interactions in the text.
    - **Techniques + Main Idea or Message:** How does the author use cause-and-effect ideas to express the main idea?
    - **Point of View + Implications:** What are the implications of the pros and cons of deforestation for humans, according to the article?
    - **Supporting Details + Main Idea or Message:** How do the details the author provides help shape your understanding of the main ideas of the article?
    - **Supporting Details + Context/Audience/Purpose:** How does the author's purpose of the article influence the details that are included?
    - **Techniques + Supporting Details:** How might the article be organized differently if the article were only about the problems with deforestation?
    - **Point of View + Supporting Details:** How do you know if the details provided are fact or opinion? How does your point of view about deforestation compare to the one expressed in this article?
    - **Techniques + Main Idea or Message:** How does the author's organization of the article into the different sections help us understand the main idea of the article?

8. Ask again: *Should we cut down trees?* Have students discuss their thoughts again, including whether or not they changed their minds and why.

Choice-Based Differentiated Products

Students may choose one of the following to complete (*Note*: Use Rubric 1: Product Rubric in Appendix C to assess student responses):

1. Find another story you have recently read or know (i.e., *The Three Little Pigs, Little Red Riding Hood, Goldilocks and the Three Bears*, etc.) or picture (illustrations, wordless picture books, primary sources) that you enjoy and make a list of the interactions the author uses to support a message. Roll the cubes or use the Literary Analysis Wheel—Primary and see how many interactions between the different story elements you can find. Make a list of the interactions and write a statement about how the interactions of different story elements help us understand the author's message.

2. Create a 3- to 4-frame comic strip that highlights the most important events in *The Great Kapok Tree* and ends with the main message.

3. Design a new cover and title for the story that use different colors that capture the mood of the story and convey the main theme.

4. Write a paragraph or record a speech that explains your position about whether or not trees should be cut down to support the needs of humans and includes relevant facts that support your position.

Opportunities for Talent Development

1. Have students research how a specific animal, such as a bee, spider, spider monkey, ladybug, mosquito, etc., impacts the ecosystem: *Create a poem, a story, or an educational poster for younger students or the community from the perspective of your selected animal explaining your importance in the ecosystem and your place in it, including what would happen if you became extinct.*

2. What lessons from *The Great Kapok Tree* are important to consider in your local community? Have students write a letter to a local leader persuading him or her to plant more trees or to reduce the number of trees or plants that might be cut down. Students should include information about the importance of interactions between humans, plants, and animals, as explained in *The Great Kapok Tree*.

Social-Emotional Connection

In *The Great Kapok Tree*, the animals worked together to convince the man to change his mind. Have students think about a time when they worked with another friend or in a group to achieve a common purpose: *What made your team success-*

ful? Create a diagram or recipe that shows characteristics of a successful team and compare this to how the animals worked together.

ELA Task

Assign the following task as a performance-based assessment for this lesson: *Write a paragraph to describe how authors use interactions to help us understand the message of a story. Use the theme in* The Great Kapok Tree *and different interactions of characters, conflict/plot, and point of view as examples. Include evidence from both the text and the images to support your response.*

Concept Connections

1. Ask: *How does the message in* The Great Kapok Tree *relate to one of the generalizations about interactions discussed earlier in this lesson?*
2. Students may record their responses on Handout 1.5: Concept Organizer. For example, students may explain that the inevitability of interactions may be seen as the man was entering the rainforest habitat and as a result of that action would have some sort of interaction with the plants and animals living there. It is not necessary for students to make connections to every generalization.

Note: You may also design a class concept map-working wall. Write the word *interactions* in the middle of the wall; write and post specific generalization statements around the word *interaction*. As the unit continues, students may add their connections from their current content to the class concept wall using sticky notes or scrap paper.

Assessment

- Examine choice-based differentiated products and rubric criteria, ELA Task responses, and/or Concept Connections. Use Rubric 1: Product Rubric to review the products.
- Have students complete an exit ticket: *In* The Great Kapok Tree, *the theme is* _____ *and the author shows us this by* _____ *(list interactions).*

Handout 1.1

Literary Analysis Cubes

Directions: Cut out each cube, fold along the lines, and glue or tape the tabs inside the cube.

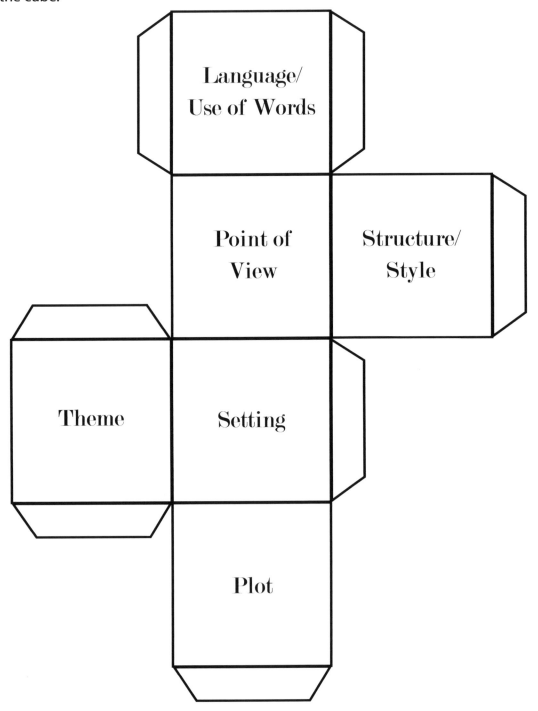

Created by Tamra Stambaugh, Ph.D., & Emily Mofield, Ed.D., 2017.

Handout 1.1, Continued

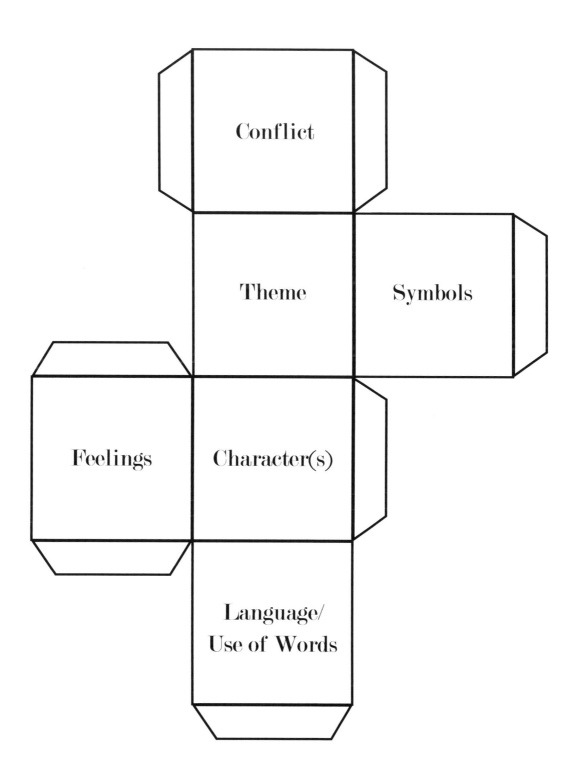

Created by Tamra Stambaugh, Ph.D., & Emily Mofield, Ed.D., 2017.

Name: _____ Date: _____

Handout 1.2
Blank Literary Analysis Wheel—Primary

Directions: Draw arrows across elements to show connections.

Text: _____

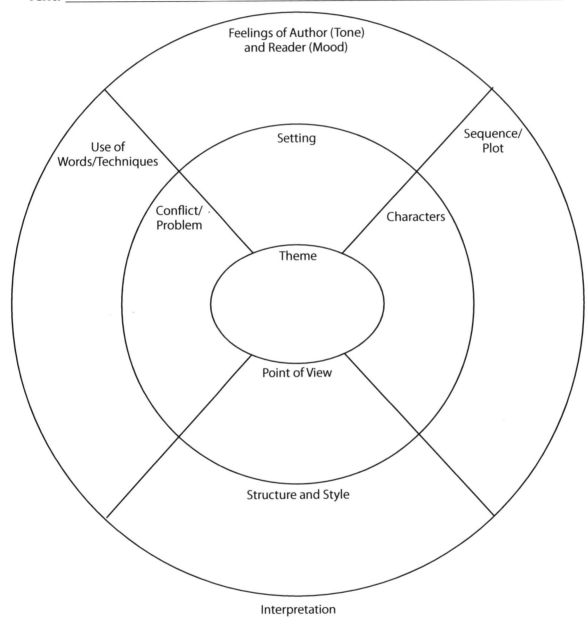

Created by Tamra Stambaugh, Ph.D., & Emily Mofield, Ed.D., 2017.

Name: _____ Date: _____

Handout 1.3
Deforestation Pros and Cons

There are 10 billion acres of forests in the world. These forests are home to millions of different plants and animals. Fifteen million acres of forests are being cut down every year in a process called *deforestation*. Should we stop quickly cutting down forests? There are both benefits and disadvantages to deforestation.

Pros

Because there are billions of acres of forests in the world, cutting some of them down makes room for our growing population. The world population is increasing and expected to reach 10 billion people by the year 2050. Even now, there are many countries that do not have enough developed space for people to live. Deforestation is a way to free up more space and allow for the development of housing. Cutting down forests also makes room for better road systems and businesses. Clearing forests makes it possible to create roads that can connect people to helpful services. In addition to developing roads in cleared forests, businesses can be created that will be good for the economy. New businesses can provide jobs that are helpful to the community.

Deforestation also creates more land that can be used for farming and agriculture. With the increasing human population, there is a greater need for food. Grazing animals, such as cows, need a lot of room to eat. Cleared forests provide grass and corn for the animals to eat, as well as space for them to graze. This also makes room to grow crops that could feed millions of people. The trees that are cut down can be used for many different helpful products, such as lumber and paper products. Through deforestation, land availability increases, and there are many ways to make that land useful. Beyond the added benefit of having more land to grow food, scientists have also been able to harvest certain plants and trees during deforestation to develop medicines. These discoveries have led to the invention of new medicine that has saved countless human lives.

Cons

Deforestation is happening at such a fast rate that, if it continues, we may not have any more forests in 100 years. We may also lose many of the plant and animal species that are native to forests. Deforestation removes the habitat for millions of birds, frogs, insects, and other creatures. Animals who typically live in forests are forced into areas that they cannot survive in. Animals may become endangered or even extinct if they do not have a safe place to live. The creatures that live in forests are important to different food chains. If insects and animals become extinct, their absence will create a chain reaction that will impact humans.

The loss of trees and plants also creates a problem for the air that we need to breathe. Plants remove carbon dioxide gases out of the air and release oxygen. If there are fewer plants to clean the air, there will be more carbon dioxide and less oxygen. Scientists study forests and develop new medicines using plants. With deforestation, people will not be able to study forests and develop new medicines. These medicines can be very helpful to humans. The loss of plants and trees also increases the risk of flooding. Plants and trees have deep roots that absorb extra ground water. If the water is not absorbed by the roots, it can flood nearby areas and impact many people.

There are environmental organizations that are working to protect forests by replanting native trees and plants. These organizations create wildlife areas that provide homes for many insects and animals.

REFERENCES

HealthResearchFunding.org. (2014). *Pros and cons of deforestation*. Retrieved from https://healthresearchfunding.org/pros-cons-deforestation

Lombardo, C. (2015). *Pros and cons of deforestation*. Retrieved from http://visionlaunch.com/pros-and-cons-of-deforestation

Wildscreen Arkive. (2017). *Reforestation*. Retrieved from http://www.arkive.org/reforestation

Name: _____ Date: _____

Handout 1.4

Blank Text Analysis Wheel—Primary

Directions: Draw arrows across elements to show connections.

Text: _____

Created by Tamra Stambaugh, Ph.D., & Emily Mofield, Ed.D., 2017.

Handout 1.5
Concept Organizer

Directions: Which generalizations are most evident in this lesson, book, story, poem, art, or problem? Write the number of the generalization(s) and evidence you have. What new generalizations or connections can you make to other concepts?

1. Interactions are inevitable.
2. Interactions allow for changes.
3. Interactions are caused by multiple influences.
4. Interactions can be positive, negative, or mutually beneficial.

	Book, Story, Poem, Art, Problem: _____	**Book, Story, Poem, Art, Problem:** _____
Interaction Generalization(s) *(Write the Corresponding Number)*		
Explanation and Evidence for the Generalizations		
Connections to Other Ideas and Concepts		

Lesson

2

Interactions Among Living and Nonliving Things: Ecosystems and Food Chains

Key Question

How do interactions between living and nonliving things impact the environment?

Objectives

Content: To analyze and interpret fiction, nonfiction, and art, students will be able to:

  ▪ cite evidence in discussion and writing to support a point of view illuminated through literature, art, or nonfiction.

To understand ecosystems, students will be able to:

  ▪ analyze how scientific elements (energy, structure, patterns, findings, etc.) interact to build understanding related to issues and problems;
  ▪ cite examples of food chains from different environments;
  ▪ demonstrate the flow of energy within a food chain;
  ▪ explain the relationship between producers, consumers, and decomposers and the sun; and
  ▪ explain the relationships and provide examples of interactions between living and nonliving things.

Process: To develop interpretation, analysis, and communication skills in the language arts, students will be able to:

  ▪ respond to an analysis of literature, nonfiction, or art by developing arguments or elaborating on explanations through writing a variety of texts (e.g., essays and paragraphs, including relevant and sufficient evidence to support claims).

To understand ecosystems, students will be able to:

  ▪ use food web models to analyze the flow of energy and the interaction among living organisms within an ecosystem; and

- create models to explain what happens to a food web when abiotic and biotic factors change.

Concept: To develop conceptual thinking about interactions in the language arts and science, students will be able to:
- explain how interactions promote change in multiple contexts across multiple disciplines;
- synthesize information from various texts, sources, and models to support generalizations about interactions; and
- examine the relationship between interactions, relationships, and change in multiple contexts.

Accelerated CCSS for ELA

- W.4.2b
- W.4.2d
- L.4.6

Accelerated NGSS

- 5-PS3-1
- 5-LS2-1

Materials

- Videos:
  - "Fabulous Food Chains: Crash Course Kids #7.1" (available at https://www.youtube.com/watch?v=MuKs9o1s8h8)
  - "Food Chains" (available at http://studyjams.scholastic.com/studyjams/jams/science/ecosystems/food-chains.htm)
  - "Abiotic and Biotic Factors" (available at https://www.youtube.com/watch?v=E1pp_7-yTN4)

- Handout 1.5: Concept Organizer
- Handout 2.1: Biotic and Abiotic Cubes (one set per group of 3–4; cut and folded into cubes in advance)
- Handout 2.2: Blank Science Analysis Wheel
- Rubric 1: Product Rubric (Appendix C)

Introductory Activities

1. Display the word *ecosystem*. Tell students that the prefix "eco-" originated from the Greek word "oikos," which means house. So "eco-" is our Earth house, or our environment. Something that is ecofriendly is good (or friendly) for the environment.

2. Ask: *If "eco-" means environment, what is an ecologist? What is ecology? What is an ecosystem?* Explain that students will be studying ecosystems, or how living things and nonliving things interact with each other.

In-Class Activities to Deepen Learning

1. Show the videos, "Fabulous Food Chains: Crash Course Kids #7.1" and "Food Chains" (see Materials list). Tell students you want them to examine how living things interact through food chains. Ask:
   - Where does all energy for living things on Earth originate? (The sun.)
   - What role do plants play in a food chain? (All transfer of energy on Earth within a food chain begins with plants.)
   - How does transfer of energy happen in an ecosystem in ways that support human life? (Energy from the sun helps with plant photosynthesis. Energy is not generated but is transferred through food chains. The sun transfers energy to plants; animals eat plants to get energy; animals eat other animals that eat plants; humans eat plants and animals to get energy.)
   - How do consumers, producers, and decomposers interact to support a healthy environment? (Students should recognize the following cycle: [1] plants, to [2] primary, secondary, and tertiary consumers, to [3] decomposers, which in turn feed plants through enriched soil.)
   - What food chains are found where you live? (Students may indicate the sun, grass, rabbit, and coyote; leaf, caterpillar, bird.) Where do decomposers fit in? (They break down decaying matter into nutrients that support more plant growth.)
   - What would happen if decomposers were not present in an ecosystem? (Students may discuss how plants may not be as healthy and things in the environment may not break down materials to support healthy life of other animals.)
   - How do consumers support decomposers? (Students may consider the parts of other animals that are not eaten and left to be broken down, as well as feces.)

- How do consumers support producers? (Students may mention animals that eat seeds and then spread them in other places when they eliminate waste.)
- How might food chains and the types of consumers, producers, and decomposers differ in different environments? (Students should recognize that forests, the arctic, the desert, and the sea have different types of food chains based on the animals that thrive there.)

2. In small groups, ask students to discuss the following question based on their understanding of the food chain and interactions among living things: *The food chain has been represented as a chain and a pyramid. Based on what you know, should the interaction among living things in a food chain be represented best as a chain, a pyramid, or a circle? Why or why not?*

3. Next, explain that these living things also interact with nonliving things. Show the video on biotic and abiotic factors (see Materials list). Ask:
   - What is the difference between biotic (living) and abiotic (nonliving) interactions in a food chain? How are both needed to maintain a healthy environment? (Sample response: If one gets out of balance, it can affect everything else. For example, too much water can drown plants, which in turn reduces the amount of food an animal has to eat, which impacts other animals.)
   - How are nonliving (abiotic) factors important to an ecosystem? (Sample response: Temperature can affect which living things thrive or die; the sun provides energy for plants; too much or not enough rain can affect the plants that live there.)
   - Based on the examples in the video, what might be an example of a biotic and abiotic interaction in your environment? (Sample response: Animals gathering near a pond to get water; birds that migrate to warmer weather; rocks as a place for lizards to find protection to survive; plants not having enough water to grow; animals that leave an area to go to a new place to find water, thus affecting the food chain.)

4. Divide students into groups of 3–4, and provide each group with the pre-made abiotic and biotic cubes from Handout 2.1 (Cubes 1–5). Ask students to roll each cube so that they have showing an example of an abiotic factor, a producer, a primary consumer, a secondary or tertiary consumer, and a decomposer. Ask them to begin with at least two of the cubes and determine the interaction. Continue to add as many cubes as possible, discussing the different interactions that might take place. (For example, if students roll *sun, grass, rabbit, fox,* and *earthworms*, they may group the sun and grass and discuss how the sun provides energy that helps the grass grow. They may

also show how the rabbit, fox, and grass interact, as the rabbit eats the grass and the fox eats the rabbit. They may discuss how the worms and the grass interact, as the worms break down nutrients in the soil, which in turn helps the grass grow.)

5. Next, explain that when a living thing's environment changes, it will adapt, move to a new location, or die. Tell students to keep their cubes and that they are going to add one more cube that changes an interaction. Distribute Cube 6 to each group. Ask students to discuss what might happen to the other living things in the environment if there were a change. (For example, if students roll *fox, rabbit, grass, earthworms,* and *water (rain/bodies of water),* as well as *increase a consumer,* they should discuss what would happen to the rabbit, grass, worms and water in an ecosystem if the fox numbers increased.)

6. As students are working on this activity, help them understand the following three ideas:
   - Living and nonliving things interact.
   - When an ecosystem gets out of balance, it affects everything else in that ecosystem.
   - When the ecosystem changes, living things adapt, die, or move to a new location.

Science Analysis

1. Explain that scientists use different processes to think about scientific phenomena and to solve problems or model how they think a solution or hypothesis might play out in real life.

2. Distribute Handout 2.2: Blank Science Analysis Wheel. If needed, briefly introduce students to the meaning behind each of the categories (i.e., cause and effect, structure and function, systems/energy and matter). *Note:* More information about the concepts from the inner circle of the Science Analysis Wheel can be found by conducting an online search for "Next Generation Science Standards Cross Cutting Concepts." Some of the NGSS concepts on the wheel are combined. Explain to students that the center of the wheel is their hypothesis, solution idea, question, or problem.

3. Guide students to understand how various elements interact to help scientists understand issues and develop solutions, grounding the analysis in the idea that interactions between living and nonliving things have an impact on ecosystems. (*Note:* If this is students' first encounter with the Science Analysis Wheel, additional modeling may be needed.)

4. Pose the following problem: *Your school needs a new gymnasium. The mayor has said that she will give you the space needed for the new gymnasium from*

government-owned land. You just have to fill in a pond and build on top of it. Based on what you know about living and nonliving interactions, what do you predict will happen as a result of this building? Use the Science Analysis Wheel to help you think through your ideas.

- **Real-World Issue or Problem:** How do people interact with the environment in positive and negative ways?
- **Center of the Wheel:** What is the impact of filling in a pond to build a gymnasium for kids?

Select from the following questions to guide students.

Simple Science Questions:

- **Systems/Energy and Matter:** How might filling in a pond impact the food chains and flow of energy of the animals and plants that live there? (Sample response: If the pond is filled in, then producers who grow in or near the pond are threatened or removed entirely from the ecosystem. The flow of energy from producers to consumers is disrupted. When producers are gone and a water source is gone, the animals that need them will leave and maybe overcrowd another place nearby or die. Animals may not have water.)

- **Evidence/Data:** What evidence or data might you need to collect to measure the effects? (Sample response: I could keep a list of animals and plants that live there before and after the building is built and see which ones live, move on, or die.)

- **Stability and Change:** What changes over time might occur within the ecosystem if we build a gymnasium over the pond? (Sample response: Removing the pond as a source of water and also as a habitat for some living organisms could change the animals that live there. This could result in additional changes to other animals and plants that relied on current animals to thrive.)

- **Cause and Effect:** What effects might filling in the pond have on the people who live nearby? (Sample response: Filling in the pond could have both negative and positive effects on the people who live nearby. Building the gymnasium could lead to healthier lives for students, but it could negatively impact them by removing a natural water source, producers who make oxygen, etc.)

- **Perspectives/Audience:** What perspectives might we consider and how are the different people/perspectives impacted? (Sample response: The people in nearby areas may see in increase in animals moving closer to their homes and new water sources, the students could be positively impacted by having a gymnasium so they will be healthier but negatively impacted over time if there is not a healthy ecosystem because there are no water sources, etc.)

■ **Modeling:** How can we model what might happen if we fill in the pond? What would your model look like? (Answers will vary, but students need to consider the food chain, animal and plant impact, and that new animals may come in while others move out. It will affect several living things. Emphasize that most land animals will move to other places or adapt. Most animals will not die. The animals in the pond, however, will die unless they are moved to another location.)

■ **Findings/Solutions:** If this is the only place to build the gymnasium, what solutions might there be to minimize the impact? What have other communities done in situations like this? (Answers will vary. You may be able to find information from news articles about other communities who have dealt with similar issues. Encourage students to brainstorm a variety of solutions and justify their solutions and impacts.)

Complex Science Questions:

■ **Systems/Energy and Matter + Stability and Change:** Based on this idea, how would changes in the flow of energy between living things and non-living things impact the environment over time? (Sample response: If the pond were filled in, the producers and prey, such as mosquitos, that live in and around the pond would not be able to thrive. This would disrupt the flow of energy as consumers and predators would have less to eat.)

■ **Stability and Change + Systems/Energy and Matter:** How will the stability of the ecosystem adapt over time once the gymnasium is built? (Sample response: Depending on the health of the ecosystem, it will adapt slowly to a new normal. New animals will move in, new plants that don't need as much water will grow as birds and other animals spread seeds, and new food chains and webs will be established.)

Afterward, ask: *What new questions do you have about ecosystems and food chains? What advice would you give the mayor and city council based on your knowledge and the information learned from completing the Science Analysis Wheel?*

Choice-Based Differentiated Products

Students may choose one of the following to complete (*Note*: Use Rubric 1: Product Rubric in Appendix C to assess student responses):

■ Watch "Climate Change: Crash Course Kids #41.2" (available at https://www.youtube.com/watch?v=SzcGTd8qWTg). Then, research another animal, such as the penguin, polar bear, etc., and examine how changes in temperature might affect its behavior. Create an infographic that illustrates your findings.

- Create a solution to the problem about building a gymnasium over a pond. Use the Science Wheel to explore whether or not your solution is doable. Don't forget to consider the perspectives of the mayor and the students as well as ecologists.
- Write a persuasive essay that explains whether ecologists should represent the food chain as a chain, a pyramid, or a circle.
- How is *The Great Kapok Tree* (from Lesson 1) part of an ecosystem? What are the living and nonliving things that interact to make the tree a vibrant place for the animals to live? (Students may need to refer back to the story and the video.) After you have identified the biotic and abiotic interactions, create a model of the kapok tree's ecosystem and the interactions that occur.
- Create a cartoon strip set within a particular ecosystem: Within the cartoon, introduce a new living or nonliving object (e.g., human, chair, car, etc.), and include the ways in which the existing living and nonliving things might interact with it. How might the new addition and the new interactions lead to changes within the ecosystem?

Opportunities for Talent Development

1. Invite a local ecologist to visit your class (in person or virtually). Have students ask the ecologist about interactions between people, plants, animals and nonliving things within ecosystems. How does an ecologist spend his or her day? What schooling or degree is required? What types of jobs exist for individuals with degrees in ecology? How do ecologists study interactions? What impact do interactions among plants, animals, and people have on ecosystems?

2. What impact does human population and building have on an ecosystem and food chains? Have students write a letter to a builder or developer, asking about his or her awareness of the interaction among living and nonliving things in the environment and how his or her building might impact that. Students can use the Science Analysis Wheel as a guide for developing their questions.

3. Have students observe an ecosystem in their local area (i.e., desert, forest, wetland, etc.) for one week: *An ecosystem must have biological (biotic/living; plants, animals and other life forms) and physical (abiotic/nonliving; soil, water, air, climate, topography, etc.) components. Keep track of both the expected and unexpected interactions observed. What impact do the animals' interactions with nature have on the ecosystem? How have humans positively or negatively impacted the ecosystem? Design a model of interactions that you observe, using arrows to show relationships.*

Social-Emotional Connection

Interactions between living and nonliving things can be positive, negative, or neutral. Tell students they have discussed how these interactions occur with plants, animals, and abiotic elements: *Think about your personal interactions with biotic (parents, friends, siblings, pets, plants) and abiotic (books, house, toys, paint) factors. How do changes in your interactions affect your mood? Create a diagram that shows your personal ecosystem.*

ELA Task

Assign the following task as a performance-based assessment for this lesson: *Explain how interactions between living and nonliving things in an ecosystem allow for change in both positive and negative ways. Include examples of food chains, as well as abiotic factors that influence these chains.*

Concept Connections

1. Add new information learned from this lesson to the generalizations about interactions on the class concept wall or to Handout 1.5: Concept Organizer. Consider making connections between living and nonliving interactions and the concept of change (change happens over time, change can be positive or negative, change can be natural or manmade, change is inevitable, and change can be orderly or random). Ask students to make a connection between interactions that occur between living and nonliving and how they lead to changes within the ecosystem.
2. Have students write a statement that includes at least two of the following words: *interactions, living, nonliving, change, ecosystem.*

Assessment

- Examine choice-based differentiated products and rubric criteria, ELA Task responses, and/or Concept Connections reflections.
- Have students select an ecosystem, such as the rainforest, forest, pond, their own backyard, etc.: *Draw a model that shows what happens to the other living and nonliving things in that ecosystem if you remove one element of that ecosystem (i.e., remove the pond, the tree, the grass) or introduce another (living or nonliving). Explain or draw how the different elements interact differently if new interactions take place within an ecosystem.*
- Have students complete an exit ticket: *Draw a model of a living and nonliving interaction, including at least three living things and one nonliving thing.*

Handout 2.1
Biotic and Abiotic Cubes

Directions: Cut out each cube, fold along the lines, and glue or tape the tabs inside the cube.

CUBE 1: ABIOTIC

Temperature
(Cold)

Soil

Water
(Rain/Bodies
of Water)

Carbon
Dioxide

Oxygen

Temperature
(Hot)

CUBE 2: BIOTIC: PRODUCERS

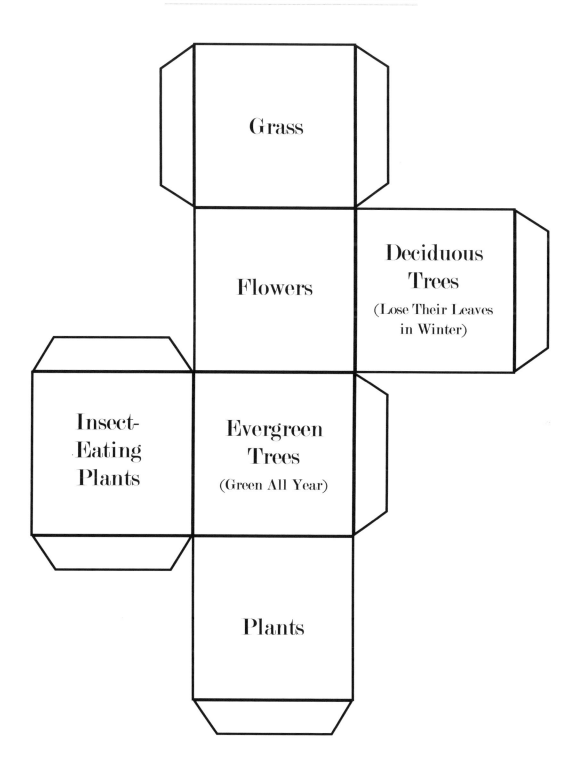

CUBE 3: PRIMARY CONSUMERS (HERBIVORES)

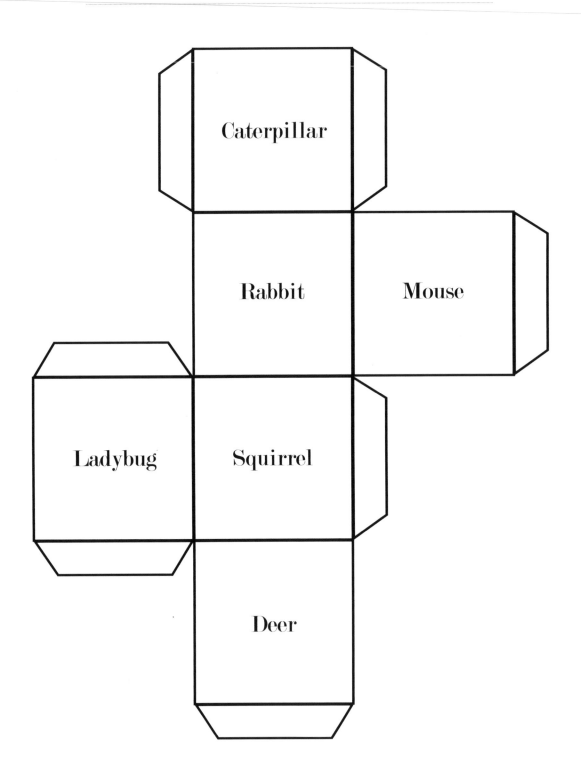

CUBE 4: SECONDARY AND TERTIARY CONSUMERS (CARNIVORES)

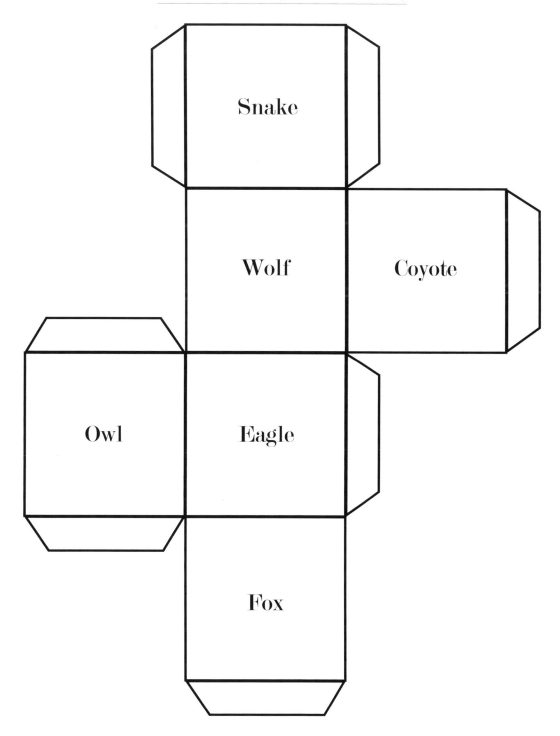

Handout 2.1, Continued

CUBE 5: BIOTIC: DECOMPOSERS

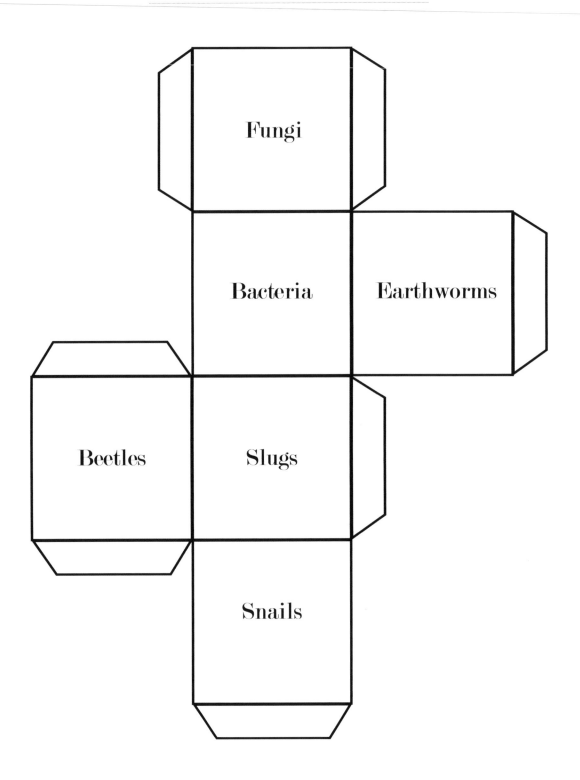

CUBE 6: CHANGING ELEMENTS

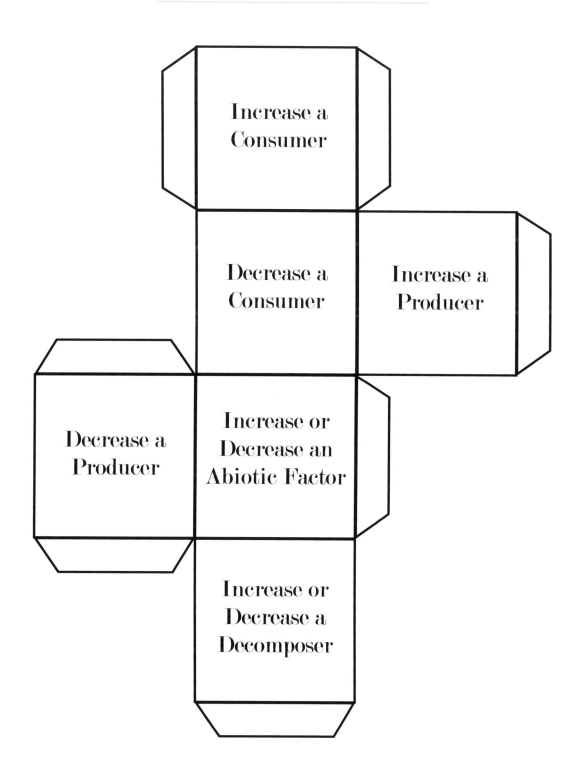

Increase a Consumer

Decrease a Consumer

Increase a Producer

Decrease a Producer

Increase or Decrease an Abiotic Factor

Increase or Decrease a Decomposer

Name: _____ Date: _____

Handout 2.2
Blank Science Analysis Wheel

Real-World Issue or Problem: _____

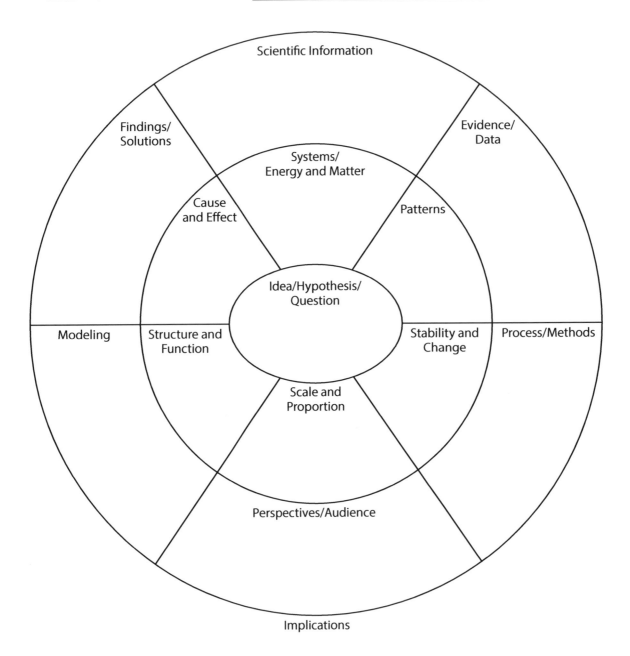

Created by Tamra Stambaugh, Ph.D., & Emily Mofield, Ed.D., 2017.

The middle section of the Science Analysis Wheel is adapted from the Next Generation Science Standards Crosscutting Concepts (National Research Council, 2012).

Lesson

Interactions and Literature: A Novel Study

Key Question

How does an author's use of character interactions develop the theme of the story?

Objectives

Content: To analyze and interpret fiction, nonfiction, and art, students will be able to:

   - evaluate how an author uses language, structure, and point of view to reveal purpose and/or advance a claim.

Process: To develop interpretation, analysis, and communication skills in the language arts, students will be able to:

   - respond to an analysis of literature, nonfiction, or art by developing arguments or elaborating on explanations through writing a variety of texts (e.g., essays and paragraphs, including relevant and sufficient evidence to support claims); and
   - use evidence to develop inferences, justify arguments, and develop claims.

Concept: To develop conceptual thinking about interactions in the language arts and science, students will be able to:

   - explain how interactions promote change in multiple contexts across multiple disciplines;
   - synthesize information from various texts, sources, and models to support generalizations about interactions; and
   - examine the relationship between interactions, relationships, and change in multiple contexts.

Accelerated CCSS for ELA

- RL.4.2
- RL.4.3
- RL.5.1
- RL.5.3

- RL.5.5
- W.4.9
- SL.5.1a
- SL.5.1c

- SL.5.1d
- L.4.6

Materials

- Student copies of *The One and Only Ivan* by Katherine Applegate
- Video: "The One and Only Ivan – Official Book Trailer" (available at https://www.youtube.com/watch?v=UtPdqV2crQ0)
- Chart paper and markers (one set per group of 3–4)
- Handout 1.5: Concept Organizer
- Handout 3.1: Story Quotes
- Handout 3.2: Blank Literary Analysis Wheel—Primary
- Rubric 1: Product Rubric (Appendix C)

Note: This lesson includes activities and questions for reading and analyzing an entire novel. Establish a timeline and specific days each week or every few days to discuss specific chapter questions, to provide feedback on students' ongoing activities, and to check for understanding. Product choices are also included for students to complete upon completion of the novel and should be considered when planning the lesson.

Introductory Activities

1. **Engage students in a quick debate:** Debate the following statements. Students can stand on opposite sides of the room to defend their point of view:
   - Friends are just as important as family.
   - Hope is more important than courage.
   - Freedom is just a state of mind.
   - Art is only created by humans.

2. Explain that these concepts will appear in the novel they will be reading, *The One and Only Ivan* by Katherine Applegate. After students read and debate each statement, tell them they will be discussing the author and the characters' points of view toward each statement as they read.

3. Watch the book trailer for *The One and Only Ivan* (see Materials list). Tell students you are going to watch the book trailer multiple times:

- The first time they watch it, tell students to look for important words and feelings. Discuss ideas, such as how the word *alone* appears to jump out and stand on its own.
- Watch the trailer again, and ask students to look for important symbols. They may notice the tire swing, representing the circular nature of no escape from the cage, or how the counting of the days slowly clicks away.
- The third time students watch the trailer, ask them to close their eyes and listen to the music. Ask them to raise their hands when they notice the change in music. Pause the video when the students raise their hands each time. Discuss what is happening and what has happened in the video based on the music: *How does the music help you think about mood? What tone does this trailer set?* (*Note*: Tone and mood may need to be defined in more detail for students: Tone is the author's attitude; mood is the reader's feeling.)

4. Distribute Handout 3.1: Story Quotes. Explain to students that these quotes are used throughout the book. Divide students into groups of 3–4. Students should paraphrase and interpret selected quotes and draw an illustration to represent the quotes (some groups may be assigned more than one quote). As students begin reading the book, explain that they will look for how these quotes are used in the story.
5. Establish a timeline for students to read the book, and explain your expectations for the novel reading, questions, and ongoing activities.

Chapter Discussion Questions

Select from the following questions for class discussion. Some may be considered as reader's response journal entries, but most are intended for class discussions, checks for understanding, and literary analysis. Selection of questions may be based on student readiness or interest with some assigned or some selected. Because there are not numbered chapters provided in the text, the following page ranges are used as markers. Note that page numbers may differ based on the edition of the book.

Pages 1–98:
1. How is Ivan's life as a gorilla different in the Big Top Mall compared to the life of gorillas in the wild?
2. How does Ivan respond to life in his cage? What does this reveal about his character?
3. How is Ivan's domain like an ecosystem? Are there any elements missing from his domain that, if added, would make it an ecosystem?

4. Revisit the interaction generalizations. Think about Ivan, Bob, Stella, and Mack. Which generalizations best fit their relationship?

5. Note how the author uses humor at various points throughout the first part of the book (e.g., Ivan's me-balls, the descriptions of Bob, etc.). How does the use of humor interact with the other realities of Ivan's situation?

6. Note the author's use of metaphors and similes throughout the book (e.g., "Stella is a mountain. Next to her I am a rock, and Bob is a grain of sand" [p. 27]). How does the figurative language enhance your understanding of the characters? The setting?

7. Reexamine the story Stella tells about Jambo. What is the significance in her telling the story? What might this tell us about what is going to happen next?

8. Ruby's arrival brings about a new series of interactions between characters, and in many ways their world within the mall is shaken up. How do Stella and Ivan initially view Ruby's arrival? How do their experiences shape their interactions with her?

Pages 99–199:

1. The claw stick serves as an important symbol in the story. How do the characters respond when it is used? How do Ivan, Ruby, and Stella use similes and metaphors to describe the claw? How does the use of those images and symbols interact in a way that helps you better understand the plot?

2. What is the purpose of Stella's death in the novel? What do we learn about Ivan's character through this event?

3. How do mental interactions (memories) allow for change? Can mental interactions allow for change? What examples from the story suggest this?

4. Ivan makes a promise to Stella that has implications for the way he thinks and acts following her death. How does Ivan change after making the promise? How do his internal/mental changes impact the ways in which he interacts with those around him?

5. What role does Julia play in motivating Ivan to keep going? What do the art supplies symbolize?

6. What is the role of Julia and George in motivating Ivan and comforting Ruby? How do their interactions impact the way that the animals see themselves? How are their interactions with the animals different from the way that Mack interacts with them? Why is it important to show humans interacting in both ways?

7. How does Ivan begin to change once he has someone to protect?

Pages 200–300:

1. How does Ivan use art to interact with people?

2. How does the community use the power of interactions to force Mack to reconsider how the animals are treated?

3. How does the general public's belief about the animals in the mall change following their interactions with Ruby and Ivan's painting on the billboard?

4. After he is brought to the room at the zoo, Ivan is isolated from the other gorillas. Even though he can see them on TV, he isn't able to interact with them for several days. What purpose does his initial isolation serve? How does Ivan approach these changes?

5. In the closing pages, Ivan continues to create art on a freshly painted wall using soft mud. In the distance, he hears Ruby's tiny trumpet and imagines her wading through the tall grass of her enclosure. How are their new ecosystems different from the ecosystem they were a part of at the mall? What impact does this change in ecosystem have on the characters?

6. How does Ivan's perception of himself change as a result of keeping his promise and joining the gorilla troop at the zoo?

7. Is this story more about friendship and helping others or the power of interactions? Support your answer with evidence from the text.

Literary Analysis

At various points in the novel, guide students through an understanding of how various literary elements interact to create meaning in the story. Use Handout 3.2: Blank Literary Analysis Wheel—Primary or the literary cubes (see Appendix A). Help students synthesize their understanding of symbols, characters, and elements discussed during chapter questions discussion (see Appendix A for additional explanation and basic explanation of literary elements).

Ask: *How does Katherine Applegate, author of* The One and Only Ivan, *use the interactions among varying literary elements to create a strong message or main idea?* Tell students they will be examining this by using the Literary Analysis Wheel—Primary (or cubes).

Simple Questions:

- **Sequence/Plot:** What is the sequence of events that leads up to ____? (Students may sequence the events leading up to milestones in the book, such as the arrival of Ruby, Stella's death, the billboard, or the move to the zoo.)

- **Structure and Style:** How is this book organized differently than other books? (Sample response: Short, unnumbered chapters make it read almost like a journal of Ivan's thoughts and daily interactions.)

- **Use of Words/Techniques:** What examples of metaphors and similes are used throughout the book? Why does the author use these (e.g., "beckons them to stop and rest like gazelles at a watering hole"; "Her voice was like the throaty bark of a dog chained outside on a cold night"; "It left a trail in its wake like a slithering blue snake"; "Stella is a mountain")? (Sample response: The author uses these to help the reader make comparisons and illustrate a point.)

- **Feelings of Author (Tone) and Reader (Mood):** How did _____ make you feel (mood)? Consider various events within the book. What words or phrases made you feel that way? (Students may feel frustrated when Stella dies because, despite Julia's efforts, Mack did not act quickly enough to save her.)

- **Setting:** What are the two main settings presented in the text, and how are they described? (Sample response: The Big Top Mall and the zoo.)

- **Characters:** Who are the characters included in the book? (Ivan, Stella, Ruby, Bob, Julia, George, and Mack.) What inference can you make about their characters based on their words or actions? (Sample response: Stella is caring because she tells stories to Ivan and comforts Ruby when she first arrives.)

- **Point of View:** Whose point of view is the poem told from? (First person—from the perspective of Ivan.)

- **Conflict/Problem:** Which types of conflict exist in the story? (Sample response: Internal—Ivan coming to terms with his identity; man vs. nature—Mack and his mistreatment of the animals; etc.)

- **Theme:** What themes are suggested in the story? What evidence from the text supports the theme? (Sample response: Themes include the importance of friends and keeping promises, identity and belonging, treatment of animals, etc.)

Complex Questions:

- **Point of View + Characters:** How does the first person point of view influence your understanding of the characters? (Sample response: The story is told from Ivan's perspective, so we understand his internal thoughts and how he interacts with other characters. We do not get to know what other characters are thinking about the situations.)

- **Use of Words/Techniques + Characters:** How did the author's use of personification influence the description of a character? (Sample response: Ivan says that Stella's eyes "hold the pale moon in them, the way a still pond holds stars," which means Stella is a character who is beautiful and calm.)

- **Characters + Conflict/Problem:** How does the development of characters influence the conflict or resolution of the conflict in the story? (Sample response: Mack becomes increasingly greedy, and as a result, Stella does not get the attention she needs; Ivan's confidence and identity change when he has someone to protect, which brings about a solution to one of the conflicts.)

- **Structure and Style + Point of View:** How does the first person narration support the writing style where sentences and fragments of paragraphs are used? How does this influence your understanding of characters as they develop? (Sample response: The first-person narration gives us insight into what Ivan is thinking. The simple sentences and shorter paragraphs reflect his train of thought as he interacts with other characters or events in the story.)
- **Setting + Conflict/Problem:** How does the setting influence the conflict? (Sample response: The description of the cages at the mall in contrast to the animals' natural ecosystems serves as a conflict in and of itself, causing the problems in the story, such as Ivan's sadness, the death of the Stella and her mistreatment, etc.)
- **Sequence/Plot + Theme:** How does the series of events leading up to Ivan and Ruby's relocation to the zoo influence themes related to identity and keeping promises? (Sample response: Ivan begins to identify as a silverback and in doing so keeps his promise to Stella.)
- **Feelings of Author (Tone) and Reader (Mood) + Use of Words/Techniques:** How does Ivan's internal dialogue at the beginning of the novel influence the way that you feel towards him? How do your feelings change as Ivan begins to interact with Stella, Bob, and others around him? (Sample response: Ivan's words that he uses to describe himself and his domain make the reader feel somewhat lonely.)

Choice-Based Differentiated Products

Students may choose or be assigned one or more of the following to complete (*Note*: Use Rubric 1: Product Rubric in Appendix C to assess student responses):

- Write a poem that relates to one of the concepts in the book, such as freedom, power, community, purpose, or interactions. Include similes or metaphors, symbols, and a conflict that has been resolved within your poem.
- Make a diorama of one scene in the story. Use details from the text to develop the scene. Turn in a written extension that includes three quotes from the text that support your interpretation of the setting, and how your diorama sets the same tone as the scene, shapes events of the plot, and affects the characters.
- Design a museum display that shows five significant artifacts from the story. Examples might include a banana, crayons, yogurt-covered raisins, peanuts, claw sticks, etc. This can be a virtual museum created using technology (e.g., PowerPoint, Prezi, etc.) or a 3-D representation. Include a written

description of the importance of each item in the story, how it affected the characters, and any symbolism associated with the artifact.

- Metaphors and similes compare two unlike objects in ways to provide a mental picture that helps us better understand an idea. Revisit some of the metaphors and similes that were used to help readers understand the ideas in *The One and Only Ivan*. Identify the two objects being compared and the mental picture it helps create. Make an illustration for the metaphors/similes. Explain how the use of metaphors and similes helps the reader better understand the issues in the text. Create your own metaphors and similes to explain your feelings or interpretation of the mood of the text.

- Create a storyboard or comic strip that imagines Ivan, Stella, and Ruby meeting in the wild. Include information that is appropriate to the habitats and behaviors of the animals in their natural environments. Explain how their interaction in the wild would be quite unique, as elephants and gorillas are not known to have positive or mutually beneficial interactions in the wild.

- Create a visual graph to represent Ivan's journey throughout the book. Label the interactions and generalizations that occur over time, as part of his journey. Add meaningful quotes at key points in your graph to convey the main message of that particular point in the journey.

Opportunities for Talent Development

- Have students read another book by Katherine Applegate (e.g., *Wishtree, Crenshaw, Home of the Brave*, etc.): *Write a letter to the author explaining how* The One and Only Ivan *or an additional book she wrote influenced you. What big lessons or ideas from the book spoke to you and influenced the ways in which you interact with the world around you? What questions would you like to ask Katherine Applegate?*

- Ask students to compare Georges Seurat's *A Sunday Afternoon on the Island of La Grande Jatte* (discussed in Lesson 4) to the novel: *What connections can you make? Create a Venn diagram that shows the similarities and differences of the messages.*

- Ask: *Is the shopping mall containment area where Ivan and his friends lived an ecosystem? Why or why not?* Have students write an opinion piece using evidence of what they know about ecosystems and include evidence from the story to support their answer.

Social-Emotional Connection

Each of the characters responded to difficult challenges they faced in different ways. Ask: *Which character responded in a way that you do when a problem occurs? Which character is least like you in regard to the way they handle problems? What can you learn from others who handle problems differently? Choose a problem you may face, and create a dialogue between you and the character that explains how each of you might handle the problem in similar or different ways. Use evidence from the story.*

ELA Task

Assign the following task as a performance-based assessment for this lesson: *How does Katherine Applegate use techniques and elements, such as similes, metaphors, symbols, and setting, to create mood (feelings a reader has)? Write three or four sentences to explain these interactions using examples from the novel.*

Concept Connections

- Revisit the interaction generalizations, and ask students to make connections from the concepts discussed in the previous lessons (e.g., ecosystem interactions, abiotic and biotic factors) to the book *The One and Only Ivan*. Develop a large concept visual map for students to link ideas between the previous lessons. Write out explanations for how concepts are related between lessons.
- Use Handout 1.5: Concept Organizer (or see Appendix B) to record how the generalizations applied to the text. For example, interactions allow for changes—the interactions between Julia and Ivan brought about a change that eventually led to his placement in a zoo. In the last box, students should relate the idea of interactions to the concept of *power* (e.g., power of fear, power of kindness, power of freedom, power of friendship).

Assessment

- Examine choice-based differentiated products and rubric criteria, and/or Concept Connections reflections.
- Have students complete an exit ticket: *Create an analogy for Ivan's character. How is Ivan like a _____? How does this analogy relate to one of the themes in the novel (e.g., importance of friends and keeping promises, identity and belonging, treatment of animals)?*

Handout 3.1

Story Quotes

Directions: On a separate sheet of paper, paraphrase and interpret a selected quote. Then, draw an illustration to represent the quote. As you begin to read the novel, *The One and Only Ivan* (Applegate, 2017), look for how these quotes are used in the story.

- "Memories are precious . . . they help tell us who we are." (p. 53)

- "Humans waste words. They toss them like banana peels and leave them to rot. Everyone knows the peels are the best part." (p. 2)

- "They think I'm too old to cause trouble. Old age is a powerful disguise." (p. 31)

- "A good zoo," Stella said, "is a large domain. A wild cage. A safe place to be. It has room to roam and humans who don't hurt." She pauses, considering her words. "A good zoo is how humans make amends." (p. 64)

- "The names are mine, but they're not me." (p. 2)

- "With enough time, you can get used to almost anything." (p. 22)

- "It's never too late to be what you might have been."—George Eliot

- "Anger is precious. A silverback uses his anger to maintain order and warn his troop of danger. When my father beat his chest, it was to say, Beware, listen, I am in charge. I am angry to protect you, because that is what I was born to do. Here in my domain, there is no one to protect." (p. 10)

Name: _____ Date: _____

Handout 3.2

Blank Literary Analysis Wheel—Primary

Directions: Draw arrows across elements to show connections.

Text: _____

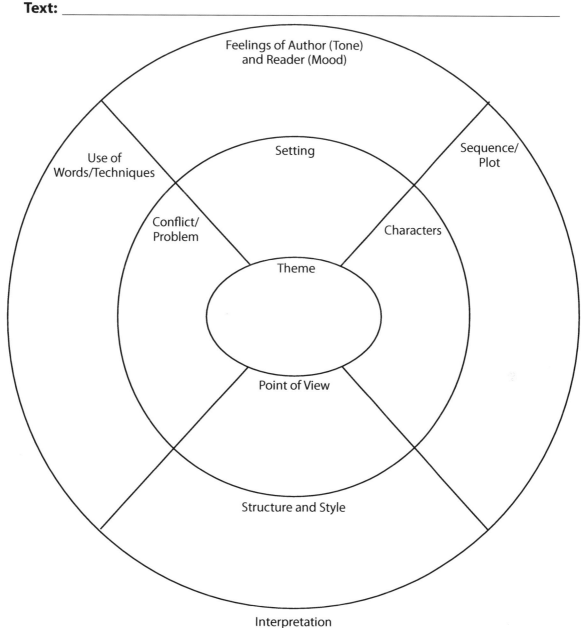

Created by Tamra Stambaugh, Ph.D., & Emily Mofield, Ed.D., 2017.

Lesson

Interactions and Perspective: Art Analysis

Key Question

How do different elements in a picture interact to create meaning?

Objectives

Content: To analyze and interpret fiction, nonfiction, and art, students will be able to:

- analyze how literary elements interact to promote meaning within a text or work of art; and
- cite evidence in discussion and writing to support a point of view illuminated through literature, art, or nonfiction.

Process: To develop interpretation, analysis, and communication skills in the language arts, students will be able to:

- respond to an analysis of literature, nonfiction, or art by developing arguments or elaborating on explanations through writing a variety of texts (e.g., essays and paragraphs, including relevant and sufficient evidence to support claims); and
- use evidence to develop inferences, justify arguments, and develop claims.

Concept: To develop conceptual thinking about interactions in the language arts and science, students will be able to:

- explain how interactions promote change in multiple contexts across multiple disciplines;
- synthesize information from various texts, sources, and models to support generalizations about interactions; and
- examine the relationship between interactions, relationships, and change in multiple contexts.

Accelerated CCSS for ELA

- W.4.2d
- W.4.3d
- SL.5.1c
- SL.5.1d

Materials

- Examples of visual illusions (to display; available at http://www.animations. physics.unsw.edu.au/jw/light/complementary-colours.htm or http://brain den.com/color-illusions.htm)
- Color wheel (to display; available online)
- *No.5/No.24* by Mark Rothko (to display; available at https://www.moma. org/collection/works/80564?locale=en)
- Examples of art by Ivan (to display; available at http://blog.thenewstribune. com/tntdiner/2008/05/29/ivan-the-gorillas-artwork-on-display-in-atlanta-restaurant)
- Examples of art by George Seurat: *The Eiffel Tower, 1889*; *Port-En-Bessin Entrance to the Outer Harbor*; *Bathers at Asnières, 1884* (to display; available online)
- *A Sunday Afternoon on the Island of La Grande Jatte* by Georges Seurat (to display; available online)
- Paintbrushes, watercolor sets, Q-tips, markers, rubber bands, and blank paper (watercolor paper, preferred) for each student
- Video: "Georges Seurat – 'A Sunday on La Grande Jatte'" (available at https://www.biography.com/video/georges-seurat-a-sunday-on-la-grande-jatte-125835843959)
- Handout 1.5: Concept Organizer
- Handout 4.1: Blank Visual Analysis Wheel
- Rubric 1: Product Rubric (Appendix C)

Note: For background information and analysis of *A Sunday Afternoon on the Island of La Grande Jatte*, visit the following websites. There are a few interpretations available online that may not be suitable for young children. Use caution if asking students to research on their own:

- "Art Review; How Seurat Worked Up to Sunday" (available at http://www. nytimes.com/2004/08/20/arts/art-review-how-seurat-worked-up-to-sun-day.html)
- "Sunday Afternoon on the Island of La Grande Jatte by Georges Seurat" (available at https://mydailyartdisplay.wordpress.com/2011/10/21/sunday-afternoon-on-the-island-of-la-grande-jatte-by-georges-seurat)
- Video: "Seurat Pointillism" (available at https://www.youtube.com/watch?v=lxMTKSp_TsY)

Introductory Activities

1. Show students examples of visual illusions (see Materials list). Ask students to try to determine what is happening and why.

2. Next, show students a color wheel (see Materials list), and explain that complementary colors are those colors that are opposite one another in a color wheel. Ask: *How does the use of complementary colors affect what we saw in the optical illusions? What do you know about mixing primary colors?* (Students should understand that red and blue make purple, etc.)

3. Share artwork by Ivan and Mark Rothko's *No.5/No.24* side by side. Do not share who painted each piece. Without providing any background information, ask students to discuss and critique the art. Ask:
   - What details do you notice in each painting?
   - What effect might each painting have on its viewer?
   - Would you consider both paintings art? Why or why not?
   - Do you think the same artist painted both paintings? Explain.

4. Explain that a famous artist named Mark Rothko did one of these paintings: The painting is housed in the Metropolitan Museum of Art and is regarded as modern art. Ivan, the real gorilla from *The One and Only Ivan,* did the other painting. Ask:
   - Which one is the art that hangs in the museum? How do you know?
   - What makes something art?
   - How might our understanding of interactions help us explain what makes something art? Solicit a variety of responses. (Students may discuss how art may try to bring about change or how interactions with art are inevitable as it is all around us.)

In-Class Activities to Deepen Learning

1. Explain: *Today we will study a piece of art to see how the artist uses interactions of color, technique, and balance in his work.* Display a variety of examples from Georges Seurat (see Materials list). Ask students to examine his art and notice interesting details about it. What do they notice about color . . . use of space? How are the pictures constructed? Ask them to look at the paintings close up and far away. What do they notice based on their perspective? (Have students focus in on the dots and the colors close up and far away.)

2. Display *A Sunday Afternoon on the Island of La Grande Jatte* by Seurat. Tell students that this is Seurat's most famous painting.

3. Divide students into groups of 3–4. Tell students they are going to play a version of "I spy" with the painting. "I spy with my little eye . . . " Students should take turns saying something different that they notice. (Students may notice a lot of dots, differently dressed people, a lot of different colors, people doing different things.)

4. After students have played the game in small groups, ask:
   - What details do you notice in the art? (Students may point out different features of the painting, including the mix of colors, different people in the painting doing different things they enjoy, people from different walks of life, a lot of pastel colors.)
   - Seurat used small dots of primary colors to create secondary colors. For example, dots of blue and red placed closely together look purple from far away. How does the interaction of color impact the mood (or how you feel as an onlooker)?
   - What ideas are represented in the art? (Sample response: Family, friendship, community, interactions of people and nature, etc.) How does the use of dots and color show this concept?

5. Provide some background information about George Seurat. The Biography.com video (see Materials list) may help introduce students to Seurat and his work. Explain that Seurat was a famous 19th-century French impressionist painter (1859–1891), who is widely known for developing and popularizing the techniques of *pointillism* (small dots of color used to create a scene, rather than brush strokes) and *chromoluminarism* (the interaction of various colored dots to create a more solid impression of color). His pointillism required a mathematical approach to painting and a strong understanding of the ways in which colors interacted with one another (Biography.com Editors, 2017; GeorgesSeurat.org, 2017).

6. Provide students with watercolor paper (or plain blank paper if necessary), watercolor paints, Q-tips, and small cups of water. Tell students they are going to create their own visual illusions, as shown earlier in the lesson. Tell them to rubber band or tape two Q-tips together, then dip one Q-tip in a primary color and the other Q-tip in a different primary color (red, yellow, or blue). They should then dab their Q-tips all over the paper. Explain that the closer together the dots are without overlapping, the better. Then try another combination of primary colors. What does their painting look like far away? Close up? How does the perspective and science of color impact what they see and how they interact with the painting?

7. Show the color wheel again. Ask students to draw something simple on their paper, like a beach ball with divided sections that show different colors. Tell them to paint a few sections of the beach ball with complementary colors

and a few sections with primary colors, using paired Q-tips (one of each color). Remind students to wait for the paint to dry before continuing with the painting process. (*Note*: If students use too much water, they won't have the same effect because the paint will bleed.) Tell them to compare their beach ball painting to Seurat's painting, which features complementary colors and color mixing. Ask: *How is this technique from your art similar to what you viewed in the Seurat paintings?*

Visual Analysis

Distribute Handout 4.1: Blank Visual Analysis Wheel. Guide students through the following questions to analyze Seurat's *A Sunday Afternoon on the Island of La Grande Jatte*. Refer students to the key question (In what ways do different elements of art, including texture, space, color, line, balance, and form, interact to create meaning?), and explain that they will learn how to use an analysis tool to see how the interactions of artistic elements and subjects of art achieve a purpose. See Appendix A for additional guidance on using the Visual Analysis Wheel. Alternatively, students may use complexity cubes to guide discussion (see Appendix A).

- **Images:** *What are the main images that you notice in the painting? Why did he choose the subjects that he did? What do you notice about the individuals drawn in the painting? How are they alike and different? What do the individuals' interactions suggest about society at the time?* Ordinary people from all walks of life are seen meeting in a "harmony of opposites."
- **Organization:** *Where are your eyes drawn to first? How do the subjects and the interaction of light impact the meaning of the work?*
- **Techniques:** *What techniques are used by the artist?* Consider how pointillism and the interaction of smaller primary-colored dots converge to form secondary colors when seen from a distance.
- **Artist's background:** *What do we know about Georges Seurat?* Remind students of your earlier discussion about his life and pointillism as well as Seurat's interest in science.
- **Emotions:** *How do you feel when you see this painting? What emotions are most present? How did the artist achieve this?*
- **Purpose:** *What do you think Seurat's purpose was in making this art?* His purpose was to paint modern people who came from all different backgrounds, some poor and some rich, some who worked and some who didn't. The park along the river was where people came to relax on Sundays, and he captured how people interacted on a Sunday afternoon. He was fascinated with the ways things interacted, especially people from different classes, and revealed this through this painting by including subjects who were from differing backgrounds.

- **Main Idea:** *Based on what we know about Seurat's purpose in painting, what do you think the main idea of this art is?* (*Note:* Seurat never revealed an intended main idea. Many critics have suggested that the painting serves as political commentary of social structures and class in France during the late 1800s. Ask students to piece together a main idea statement about interactions based on what they learned in the previous question.)
- **Point of View:** *What is Seurat's point of view about the painting?* Seurat was fascinated by encounters among opposites—city and farm, wealthy and poor—who can be seen spending a Sunday afternoon at the park.
- **Evaluation:** *Do you like this art? Why or why not?* Students may explain a variety of feelings.
- **Concept Connection:** *How does this painting apply to a generalization about interactions? What other concepts are presented (i.e., community, balance)?* Explain that interactions happen in art as well. Colors and perspectives in a painting may interact to create a message. Discuss the following interactions between varying components of the Visual Analysis Wheel:
  - **Images + Techniques:** How to the interactions of multiple colors through pointillism impact the image?
  - **Purpose + Artist Background:** How might Seurat's background influence the purpose for painting a variety of people?
  - **Point of View + Technique:** How does the technique of applying the different combinations of individual dots to form a unified color help us understand what he might be saying about interactions? (Individual people can come together and be unified or interact in positive ways.)

Ask students what other interactions they notice. Have them share with a partner and then discuss as a class.

Choice-Based Differentiated Products

Students may choose one of the following to complete (*Note:* Use Rubric 1: Product Rubric in Appendix C to assess student products):

1. Create your own piece of art that uses pointillism and portrays the concept of interactions, community, or change. Explain how the artistic elements, such as your use of color, dots, and perspective, interact in order to create a message within the art. Write an artist statement about your work that includes how the interactions within your creation show your purpose and main idea.
2. Select two or three of the subjects depicted in *A Sunday Afternoon on the Island of La Grande Jatte*, and create a poem or short story that imagines

their interactions. Use detail to paint a narrative, using words instead of colors. What are the backgrounds of the individuals, and how did they come to end up at La Grande Jatte on that special Sunday? When they interact with the other subjects, think about their interaction and whether it is positive, negative, or mutually beneficial.

Opportunities for Talent Development

- Seurat, like other well-established painters, used interactions of colors and space to convey mood and feelings within art. Provide students with the same picture (*A Sunday Afternoon on the Island of La Grande Jatte*) in duplicate, one in black and white and the other in color. Ask students to share each of the individual images with individuals (parents, other teachers, peers), and ask them what sort of mood the image creates or how the use of color makes them feel. Have students complete a brief write-up or participate in a brief discussion that explores their findings.

- Have students research famous wildlife photographers by doing a simple online search for "best wildlife photographers" and examining their photos: *What makes the photos powerful? Select one of the photographers, and learn about why he or she chose to take pictures of animals and what message he or she wants to convey. Create a mini-museum exhibit that showcases his or her work and explains its purpose. Include at least three facts about animal interactions and what you have learned about visual analysis.*

- Ask students to create a poster or ad that explains what makes something art and includes criteria they think are relevant. They can use the examples from Rothko and Ivan, as well as others they may have found.

Social-Emotional Connection

Georges Seurat took more than 2 years to create his masterpiece. That shows a lot of perseverance, hard work, and research: *What is the role of hard work, studying, and persevering on your success in school? Are hard work and perseverance more or less important than being smart or talented? Why or why not? Create a note to your future self to explain your thinking. Use examples from Seurat's life and others in your response.*

Concept Connection

Have students reflect in writing or discussion: *How does Seurat's art relate to one of the generalizations about interactions discussed earlier in this unit?* Students may record relevant responses on Handout 1.5: Concept Organizer or add to the class concept wall. They may notice that the clustering of primary colors (blue and red) makes part of the painting appear purple at a glance. In a way, the pairing of colors can be positive, or in this case, mutually beneficial. It is not necessary for students to make connections to every generalization.

Assessment

- Assess student learning by examining choice-based differentiated products and rubric criteria, and/or Concept Connections reflections.
- Have students complete an exit ticket: *How do interactions among colors and images help us understand an artist's message?*

Name: _____ Date: _____

Handout 4.1

Blank Visual Analysis Wheel

Directions: Draw arrows across elements to show connections.

Art Piece: _____

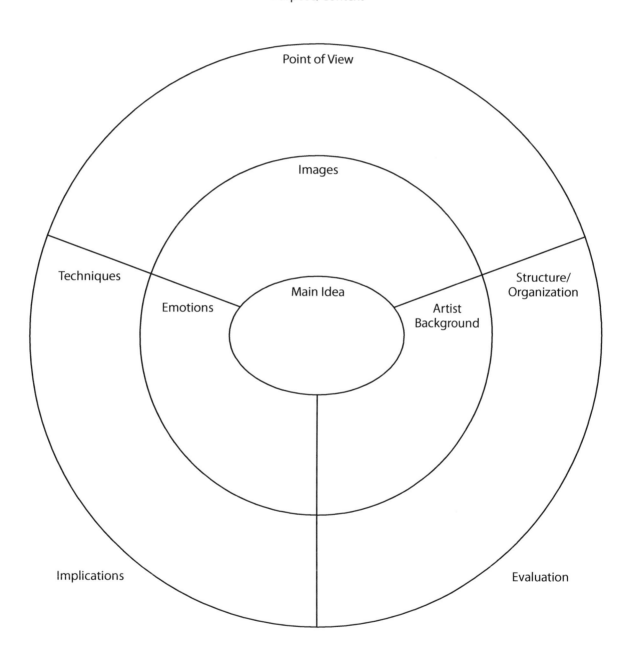

Purpose/Context

Point of View

Images

Techniques

Emotions

Main Idea

Artist Background

Structure/ Organization

Implications

Evaluation

Created by Tamra Stambaugh, Ph.D., & Emily Mofield, Ed.D., 2015.

Lesson

5

Interactions and Balance:
Simulating Ecosystems

Key Question

How do interactions among living things help support balance in ecosystems?

Objectives

Content: To analyze and interpret fiction, nonfiction, and art, students will be able to:

- cite evidence in discussion and writing to support a point of view illuminated through literature, art, or nonfiction.

To understand ecology, students will be able to:

- synthesize information to explain how interactions in an environment among living things bring about change;
- analyze how scientific elements (energy, structure, patterns, findings, etc.) interact to explain or solve an issue or problem; and
- analyze the relationship between the flow of energy and the number of organisms at each level of the food web within an ecosystem.

Process: To develop interpretation, analysis, and communication skills in the language arts, students will be able to:

- use evidence to develop inferences, justify arguments, and develop claims.

To apply knowledge of ecosystems, students will be able to:

- create a model using a computer simulation to evaluate the flow of energy and interactions among living organisms within a food web; and
- use evidence to develop conclusions about the flow of energy and the need for balance among organism populations.

Concept: To develop conceptual thinking about interactions in the language arts and science, students will be able to:

- explain how interactions promote change in multiple contexts across multiple disciplines;
- synthesize information from various texts, sources, and models to support generalizations about interactions; and
- examine the relationship between interactions, relationships, and change in multiple contexts.

Accelerated CCSS for ELA

- W.4.2d
- W.4.3d

- SL.5.1d
- SL.5.2

- L.4.6

Accelerated NGSS

- 3-LS2-1

Materials

- Blank sheets of paper (one per student)
- Videos:
  - "Food Webs: Crash Course Kids #21.2" (available at https://www.youtube.com/watch?v=Vtb3I8Vzlfg)
  - "Food Webs" (available at http://studyjams.scholastic.com/studyjams/jams/science/ecosystems/food-webs.htm)

- Student computer and Internet access
- Ecosystem simulations:
  - "Mountain Scramble" (available at http://pbskids.org/plumlanding/games/ecosystem/mountain_scramble.html)
  - "Jungle Jeopardy" (available at http://pbskids.org/plumlanding/games/ecosystem/jungle_jeopardy.html)
  - "Make a Mangrove" (available at http://pbskids.org/plumlanding/games/ecosystem/make_a_mangrove.html)
  - "Feed the Dingo" (available at http://pbskids.org/plumlanding/games/ecosystem/feed_the_dingo.html)

- Handout 1.5: Concept Organizer
- Handout 5.1: Ecosystem Simulation Recording Sheet
- Rubric 1: Product Rubric (Appendix C)

Introductory Activities

1. Show the videos about food webs (see Materials list).
2. Ask:
   - What is a food web?
   - What is the difference between a food web and a food chain?
   - How are living things connected in the environment? (Sample response: They depend on each other for food, shelter, and survival.)
   - What is the difference between consumers, producers, and decomposers? What role does each play in an ecosystem?
   - Do all ecosystems have to have consumers, producers, and decomposers? (Sample response: Yes, if they maintain balance, this is necessary.)
   - Why does the narrator in the video "Food Webs: Crash Course Kids #21.2" say that food webs are delicate? (Students should discuss the dependence on different living things to maintain balance; interdependence of different species on each other.)
   - If the environment of a living thing changes, what happens to the other animals and plants within that environment? (Sample response: They adapt, move to another place, or die.)
   - What happens when organisms within a food chain or a food web die? How does this impact the overall ecosystem?

In-Class Activities to Deepen Learning

1. Explain that students are going to simulate an ecosystem and examine how plants and animals in a food chain and food web interact and get their energy. Distribute Handout 5.1: Ecosystem Simulation Recording Sheet.
2. Tell students they are going to select a specific ecosystem to simulate using a computer program. Assign or allow students to select one of the games/environments (mountain, jungle, mangrove, outback; see Materials list).
3. Students can work independently or in groups of 2–3 to complete the ecosystem challenges as listed on the handout. They should conduct the simulations multiple times as indicated. (*Note*: Be sure to have each ecosystem represented by at least one group of students.)
4. After there has been ample time for investigation and exploration, discuss the following questions:
   - What did you have to do to keep your ecosystem alive? What lessons did you learn about how living things interact to maintain balance?
   - What interactions took place between the producers (plants) and consumers (animals) in your environment? How did you try to restore balance to your ecosystem? (Sample response: There had to be more

producers and prey than consumers and predators, with balance being restored by replacing those organisms that are lower in the food web.)

■ How can stability be reached in an ecosystem, based on your models? (Sample response: There need to be enough producers and consumers for animals to eat.)

■ What has to be in place for an ecosystem to maintain healthy organisms? (Sample response: Balanced species populations, greater number of producers than consumers, etc.)

■ How did the interactions among various animals allow for stability or change? (Sample response: If there was enough food for all of the animals, the ecosystem could remain alive and prosper; if a food source started to run out, it affected all of the other animals and changed the look of the environment [i.e., no more trees or certain animals].)

■ How did the transfer of energy from one species to another affect your environment? (Sample response: They relied on each other for food or they became weak or died off.)

■ Based on the models, what do you think would happen if we removed all of the producers in your ecosystem? (Sample response: There wouldn't be any food for other animals, and everything would eventually die out or move away in search of other food.)

■ What would happen if we introduced too many consumers? (Sample response: They may compete for food and eventually some may starve or leave.)

■ Simulations are imitations of real-life situations or processes. How did this simulation help you understand the interaction between different food webs and living things?

■ What did this simulation not take into account in terms of ecosystems and the interaction of living organisms? (Sample response: There was no human interaction or intervention in the ecosystem; no invasive species were present; no animals died from disease; decomposers were not considered; no natural population increases occurred; and there were no abiotic interactions, such as temperature changes, water changes, etc.)

■ What questions do you still have, or what new questions were created about ecosystems and the interactions of living organisms within their environment and their specific food webs?

■ What did you need to consider in the simulation in order to maintain a healthy ecosystem for more than 2 days? (Sample response: More plants and herbivores than carnivores and omnivores; the flow of energy required more producers and more primary consumers than secondary consumers, etc.)

■ Were there any differences in the simulation, based on which environment you worked in (e.g., mangrove, outback)? Explain.

Choice-Based Differentiated Products

Students may choose one of the following to complete (*Note*: Use Rubric 1: Product Rubric in Appendix C to assess student products):

■ Apply the Science Analysis Wheel to a problem you encountered from your simulation that you would like to investigate more deeply (e.g., animals were eating plants faster than they could grow; there were too many carnivores that were eating the other animals). Consider how the elements of the Science Analysis Wheel interact to help you examine your problem.

■ Look up examples of different ecosystems, and create a flowchart of interactions that would be true whether the setting was in the desert, the North Pole, or the ocean. Write a title for your flowchart.

■ Create an argument or model/diagram that shows why you need a variety of living things within an environment for it to be healthy. Be sure to include what would happen if you didn't have variety. Write a statement that explains why a variety of plants and animals are needed to maintain a healthy environment.

Opportunities for Talent Development

■ Ask students to think about animals or insects in their area or places they have visited: *How do they contribute to the ecosystem in positive ways? Create a web that shows the animals' unique ecosystem. Design their food chain and food web as part of your drawing. (Students may mention bees that pollinate flowers, other insects and animals that eat mosquitos, the reintroduction of the wolf population in Yellowstone national park that controls bison herds from overpopulation, ladybugs that eat insects that kill crops, etc.)*

■ Have students visit the website of a local or national park: *What conservation efforts are in place to protect the ecosystem? Write a letter to one of the park rangers explaining what you know about ecosystems and how his or her work connects with what you are learning about interactions among plants and animals.*

Social-Emotional Connection

Ecosystems need to maintain balance in order to thrive. This means having the proper mix of consumers, producers, decomposers, and nonliving things, such as sunlight, temperature, and water. Ask students: *Think about your life. What do you need (besides food and water) in order to maintain a healthy balance so that you are a good student and balanced person? Create a 3-day schedule that shows what your personal "ecosystem" would look like if in balance. (Consider sports you like, time to yourself to read, time with family or friends, etc.)*

ELA Task

Assign the following task as a performance-based assessment for this lesson: *How do living things in an ecosystem maintain balance? Write an explanation in a paragraph or draw a diagram.*

Concept Connections

1. Revisit the interaction generalizations, and ask students to make connections from the concepts discussed in the previous lessons, which focused on *The Great Kapok Tree* and ecosystems. Add to the large concept visual map for students to link ideas between the previous lessons. Write out explanations for how concepts are related between lessons.

2. Use Handout 1.5: Concept Organizer (continued from earlier lessons or see Appendix B) to record how the generalizations applied to the simulation or their work on the Science Analysis Wheel. For example, interactions are caused by multiple influences—the interactions between producers and consumers in an ecosystem require a delicate balance of a number of species populations. In the last box, students should relate the idea of interactions to the concept of *change* (e.g., change in populations, change in food chains/webs, change in habitats, etc.).

Assessment

■ Assess student learning by examining choice-based differentiated products and rubric criteria, ELA Task responses, and/or Concept Connections reflections.

■ Have students complete an exit ticket: *Design a model that shows interactions between producers, consumers, and decomposers in an environment. Then, change one of those interactions, and explain what happens. Use scientific language.*

Handout 5.1
Ecosystem Simulation Recording Sheet

Directions: Pick one of the four environments—mountain, jungle, mangroves, or outback—and open the simulation. Follow the directions provided in the simulation, completing the following trials. Then, answer the reflection questions at the end of the handout. When you have completed the handout, work with a classmate who completed a different simulation and compare your findings.

Trials

Trial 1: *The goal of the simulation is to create a healthy ecosystem that can survive for 12 days. The interaction of plants and animals requires you to understand the balance that exists between food webs and the way in which energy flows in a system. For this trial, explore what happens when you add the different living organisms, keeping in mind that you can add more than one of the same organism and that you may run out of certain living things.*

Reflection A: What did your ecosystem require to have healthy consumers?

Reflection B: What caused your ecosystem to have organisms that were 'less healthy' at the end of the day?

Handout 5.1, Continued

Reflection C: Other observations or questions you have:

Trial 2: *During this 12-day period, select one producer (plant), one primary consumer (e.g., ant or mosquito), and one secondary consumer (hawk, heron, badger, etc.) that you consistently add each day. You are only adding these living organisms to your ecosystem, no others.*

Producer I Added: _____

Primary Consumer I Added: _____

Secondary Consumer I Added: _____

Reflection A: What needs to be in place so that organisms at all three levels of the food web survive?

Handout 5.1, Continued

Reflection B: Did limiting your organisms to only three help or hurt your ecosystem? Why do you think that may be?

Reflection C: Is it better for ecosystems to have more or less variety of plants and animals, based on your findings?

Trial 3: *During this 12-day period, find out what happens if you add too many of one thing (i.e., consumers, producers, decomposers) and few of the other living things.*

Number of Producers I Added: _____

Number of Consumers I Added: _____

Number of Decomposers I Added: _____

(This number is the total of each added overall; not different species.)

Handout 5.1, Continued

Reflection A: How does too many of one living thing and not enough of the other impact the ecosystem? What happens?

Reflection B: How is the flow of energy and the food chain affected when there is an overpopulation of one living thing and not enough of another? Sketch a diagram that shows the effects.

Trial 4: *Your goal in this final simulation is to keep all of your organisms in good health from start to finish. You need to create an ecosystem that keeps all required species alive for at least 3 days. This means that all living things should be added no later than Day 9. Keep track of the organisms that you add below. If you fail, and one of your plants or animals becomes "less healthy," begin the simulation again, taking into account what needed to be in place for the organism to stay healthy (e.g., the ants became less healthy because there was not enough spinifex grass for them to eat).*

Organisms I Added:

Name: _____ Date: _____

Reflection A: What lessons did you learn when trying to maintain healthy organisms within your ecosystem?

Reflection B: Which organism or organisms were added most frequently? What does that say about ecosystems in general?

Reflection C: Is there a better order in which to add producers, consumers, and decomposers in order to maintain a healthy ecosystem? Explain.

Name: _____ Date: _____

Reflection Questions

Directions: Answer the following questions. You can use the back of this handout or a separate sheet of paper if needed.

1. What did this simulation not take into account in terms of real-life ecosystems and the interactions of living organisms?

2. What ecological patterns did you notice across each of the simulations?

3. What were some of the cause-and-effect relationships you noticed with producers, consumers, and decomposers?

4. How can stability be reached in an ecosystem? What has to be in place for an ecosystem to maintain healthy organisms?

5. What questions do you still have about ecosystems and the interactions of living organisms within their environment and their specific food webs?

Lesson

6

Interactions Through Words and Images: Poetry Analysis

Key Question

What impact does the author's intentional interaction of words and images have on the meaning of a piece of literature or art?

Objectives

Content: To analyze and interpret fiction, nonfiction, and art, students will be able to:

- analyze how literary elements interact to promote meaning within a story or poem;
- cite evidence in discussion and writing to support a point of view or main idea illuminated through literature, art, or nonfiction; and
- evaluate how an author uses language, structure, and point of view to reveal purpose and/or advance a claim.

Process: To develop interpretation, analysis, and communication skills in the language arts, students will be able to:

- respond to an analysis of literature, nonfiction, or art by developing arguments or elaborating on explanations through writing a variety of texts (e.g., essays and paragraphs, including relevant and sufficient evidence to support claims); and
- use evidence to develop inferences, justify arguments, and develop claims.

Concept: To develop conceptual thinking about interactions in the language arts and science, students will be able to:

- explain how interactions promote change in multiple contexts across multiple disciplines;
- synthesize information from various texts, sources, and models to support generalizations about interactions; and

▧ examine the relationship between interactions, relationships, and change in multiple contexts.

Accelerated CCSS for ELA

▧ RL.4.1

▧ RL.4.3

▧ RL.4.5

▧ RL.5.2

▧ RL.5.5

▧ RI.5.9

▧ W.4.2d

▧ W.4.3d

▧ W.4.9

▧ SL.5.1a

Materials

▧ *Surprised!* by Henri Rousseau (to display; available online)

▧ Handout 1.5: Concept Organizer (continued from previous lessons or see Appendix B)

▧ Handout 6.1: Ecology Poems

▧ Handout 6.2: Blank Literary Analysis Wheel—Primary

▧ Rubric 1: Product Rubric (Appendix C)

Introductory Activities

1. Ask students: *If you were to create a symbol that expresses an idea about animals interacting with their environment, what would that symbol be? Why? We learned in an earlier lesson that artists use interactions within their work (through light, shapes, color, style) to convey a message. How does your symbol show these interactions?* Allow students time to discuss a symbol. (Students may equate a set of gears as a symbol of ecosystem or a painting that incorporates a variety of colors to create an image in the same way that an ecosystem works to create balance.)

2. Display *Surprised!* by Henri Rousseau. Divide students into three groups: artist, ecologist, and poet. Tell students they are going to pretend to be an artist, an ecologist, or a poet, depending upon their assigned group. Ask them to talk about what they see in the painting based on their perspective.

3. Afterward, explain that students will be reading various poems about animals and their interactions within their environments and may write from various perspectives.

Read Texts

Distribute Handout 6.1: Ecology Poems. Ask students to read aloud the suggested poems and discuss initial impressions of images, ideas, and emotions. Guide students to understand how the interactions of elements within the poem (especially the use of words, mood, symbols, etc.) help convey the poem's meaning. (*Note*: The content of the suggested poem "A Series of Deaths" centers around predators and prey within a food web. A worm is eaten by a mole, who is eaten by a hawk, who is shot by a hunter, etc. If your students are uncomfortable with this content, an alternative poem focusing on ecological themes can be used in substitution.)

Discuss each poem as follows:

"In the Leafy Forest of Green" by Alexandria Junker

1. What makes this poetry? Does the rhyming pattern stay the same throughout? Why is this important?
2. How is the predator in the poem described? What might the predator be, based on the evidence? (Students may suggest that it is a bear or a wolf, based on the descriptions provided. Encourage debate based on evidence sourced from the poem and background knowledge that may have been used when making their inference.)
3. How do the subjects of the poem fit in to a particular food web, and what impact do the predator and prey interactions have on the ecosystem?
4. What impact does the repetition of the line "In the leafy forest of green" have on your understanding of the setting and the mood that the author has set?
5. Explore the use of punctuation in the poem and the way that the author uses commas to break up the sentences. Why do you think the author did this? Look specifically at the lines that read, "I see a flash, a lash, a jolt, / I give a splash, a crash, a bolt . . . "
6. What are the major concepts or ideas expressed in the poem? Literature, including poetry, reflects the human experience. What might the author want readers to consider about life?
7. How is the concept of interactions reflected in the poem?

"A Series of Deaths" by Michael Lindy

1. How does your previous learning on producers, consumers, decomposers, and food webs help you understand this poem?
2. What interactions take place within this poem, and how are they viewed as positive or negative depending on the role of the subject (e.g., the mole as both predator and prey might view killing the worm as a positive interaction, while the worm might view being eaten by the hawk as a negative one)?
3. What examples of figurative language are present in the poem, and how do they impact the setting or conflict within the poem?

4. Why does the author begin and end the poem with nearly identical stanzas? What ecology-focused message is the author attempting to get across to the audience?

5. What examples of alliteration can be found in the poem? How does alliteration in poetry impact the rhythm? How does the specific use of certain letter repetition help create mood or tone? (Sample response: Alliteration can be found in the line "swoosh and scream and several scratches." The repetition of the hard "S" creates a mood grounded in fear.)

6. Where in the poem do you notice a shift in the mood (the way that the reader feels)? How did the author use language to make this shift happen?

7. What are the major concepts or ideas expressed in the poem? Literature, including poetry, reflects the human experience. What might the author want readers to consider about life? How is the concept of interactions reflected in the poem?

8. In what ways is this poem different from the first poem? (*Note*: Make sure students take note of the varied structure, emphasis on figurative language, etc.)

Literary Analysis

Guide students to understand how various literary elements interact to create meaning in the poem. Use Handout 6.2: Blank Literary Analysis Wheel—Primary. Consider using the literary cubes to ask questions about multiple elements (see Appendix A). The following questions may be used to lead discussion. Ask: *How do authors use words to interact with their audience?* Students should draw arrows (if using the wheel) to show connections.

1. **Setting + Feelings of Author (Tone) and Reader (Mood):** How does the setting influence the mood of the poem?

2. **Use of Words/Techniques + Theme:** How do the metaphors, similes, images, or symbols help us understand the author's message?

3. **Structure and Style + Setting:** What are the specific figurative writing techniques used by the author? How do these influence the audience's understanding of the setting?

4. **Conflict/Problem + Characters:** How does the author establish conflict in the poem? In what ways does the conflict reflect an interaction between animals and nature or animals and humans? What evidence from the poem reveals this?

In-Class Activities to Deepen Learning

1. Ask students to write their own series of 3–5 poems about some of the animals discussed so far in this unit or one of their favorite animals (gorillas, elephants, animals reflected in *The Great Kapok Tree*, etc.). One of their poems should consist of multiple stanzas that detail their animals' interactions with their environment, food webs, or humans. Students can decide whether the interactions are positive, negative, or mutually beneficial. The content of their poems should be scientifically sound. Another poem can be any style that they choose (haiku, acrostic, limerick, etc.).

2. Ask students to create a piece of art for one of the poems read. They should focus on illuminating main images, ideas, and emotions of the poetry within the art. Their art must reflect the interaction mentioned in their poem.

Choice-Based Differentiated Tasks

Students may choose one of the following to complete (*Note*: Use Rubric 1: Product Rubric in Appendix C to assess student products):

- Explain the meaning of a poem through a movie or series of photos. Select a poem about an animal (from the lesson or another source). Using Movie Maker, iMovie, or other software, include images and music that relate to the poem's message.
- Write a poem that reflects your understanding of food webs or food chains. Include scientific facts as well as metaphors or similes to convey your message.
- What if Julia from *The One and Only Ivan* wrote a poem about the animal interactions that she observed in the Big Top Mall? Write a poem from her perspective that captures the interactions and the mood at various points in the story and includes the concept of ecosystems.
- Create a two-page dialogue between a literary author and an artist that explains how they use interactions in either words or pictures to convey a message and includes specific examples from a piece of art, poem, or story you know.

Opportunities for Talent Development

- How do artists and poets convey messages in different and similar ways? Have students create a Venn diagram that shows artists' and poets' similarities and differences in interpretation.
- Ask: *Students wrote the poems in this lesson. What is your talent, and how might you share it with others? What interactions would be necessary for*

you to share your talent with others (i.e., modeling your dancing, explaining artistic techniques, listening to the notes you play, etc.) Create a handout or guide that expresses your understanding of how interactions are used to develop an individual's talent within your area (i.e., drawing, sculpting, musical instruments, raising plants, etc.).

Social-Emotional Connection

Ask: *What is the role of emotion in visual art and literary art? How do artists or authors develop emotion?* Have students create a poster that explains how emotion is conveyed in art and literature and why this is important.

ELA Task

Assign the following task as a performance-based assessment for this lesson: *Compare and contrast the main ideas in "In the Leafy Forest of Green" to "A Series of Deaths." Use evidence from the text to support your ideas in a paragraph or two.*

Concept Connections

1. Use Handout 1.5: Concept Organizer (continued from previous lessons or see Appendix B) to guide students to understand how the generalizations related to the concept of interactions relate to the poetry introduced in this unit. For example, interactions can be positive, negative, or mutually beneficial. The circle of life and food web connections presented in both of these poems are interactions that, depending on the position of the living organism as predator or prey, can be seen as positive or negative.
2. Revisit the class concept generalization map. Ask students to make connections between this lesson and other ideas from previous lessons. Use arrows and words to illustrate relationships.

Assessment

- Assess student learning by examining choice-based differentiated products and rubric criteria, ELA Task responses, and/or Concept Connections reflections.
- Ask students to change the ecosystem or food web of one of the poems studied in the lesson and explain how it would affect the mood and/or use of language.
- Have students complete an exit ticket: *In this lesson, poets use the following techniques and interactions _____ to convey the message of _____.*

Handout 6.1
Ecology Poems

"In the Leafy Forest of Green" by Alexandria Junker

Stormy gray and green,
I'm stocky, sneaky, and keen,
Scrabbling paws through emerald pools,
Silver fish and foliage cool,
I stalk prey that has been seen,
In the leafy forest of green.
I see a flash, a lash, a jolt,
I give a splash, a crash, a bolt,
For that shiny fish I see in the water,
I slither in scooping for my next slaughter,
WHIP! I hook the wriggling fish on my claw,
After shooting down the stream,
In the shadowy shade of trees and jade,
A hardy fish with meat so lean,
In the leafy forest of green.
I sniff the damp and fishy scents,
I smell my fuzzy pelt,
My winter coat is thick and downy,
But in summer it's thin like felt.
I tap the water's surface,
I wait on water's edge,
I strike at swarming fish,
Beneath the rocky ledge,
Muddy marsh engulfs my claws and spreads over my bristly toes,
I wade through waters clear and cold,
Washing mud drops off my nose,
In the leafy forest of green,
Where the green fern lives and grows.

Note: Originally published in *Creative Kids* magazine, Spring 2013. Reprinted with permission of Prufrock Press.

Name: _____ Date: _____

"A Series of Deaths" by Michael Lindy

There was once a worm munching on
   soil and litter
And the bones of those long dead
As he was munching, he had a
   strange thought
One that was filled with dread
He thought, "One may fight and twist
   and bend
But Death always wins in the end."

As the little worm was munching and
   thinking
He was madly mauled by a mole
The mole thought of his food piled
   high
And said, "With these full stores and
   my claws like drills
I will go through many a night
Sleeping without worry or fright."

But it was not cold or fright that took
   the mole,
But rather a swooping hawk
And with a swoosh and scream and
   several scratches
He had not even the time to gawk
The hawk cried, "Behold, I am the
   wind and king of the skies,
And my talons pierce my prey like
   arrows!"

But as the prideful hawk sang his
   song
A bullet pierced his chest
A hunter hoisted the hunted hawk
   and proclaimed
"With my cunning and guns I am an
   unstoppable mountain
No foe can beat me and no beast can
   slay me
For I am too smart, you see."

But not all killers are big and strong
And death can find even the bold
So the man was not slain by beast or
   man
But rather by a very bad cold
The burdened man was buried briefly
Before a worm intruded sneakily

The worm started munching on soil
   and litter
And the bones of those now dead
As he was munching, he had a
   strange thought
One that was filled with dread
He thought, "One may fight and twist
   and bend
But Death always wins in the end."

Note: Originally published in *Creative Kids* magazine, Summer 2012. Reprinted with permission of Prufrock Press.

Handout 6.2

Blank Literary Analysis Wheel—Primary

Directions: Draw arrows across elements to show connections.

Text: _____

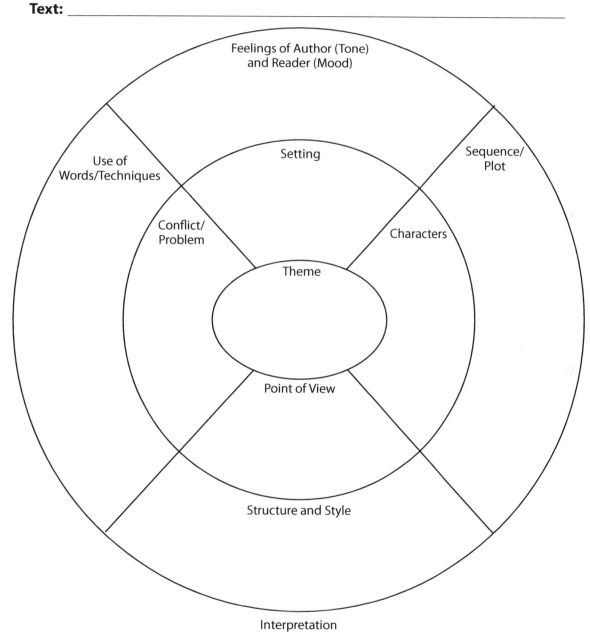

Created by Tamra Stambaugh, Ph.D., & Emily Mofield, Ed.D., 2017.

Lesson

7

Interactions and Invasive Species: Overpopulation of Wild Boars

Key Question

What impact does an imbalance or an over-/underpopulation of one species have on an ecosystem?

Objectives

Content: To understand ecology, students will be able to:

- synthesize information to explain how interactions in an environment among living things bring about change;
- analyze the relationship between population growth in one species and the impact on other living things;
- explain and demonstrate how natural and manmade changes in ecosystems lead to positive or negative changes for living organisms; and
- analyze how scientific concepts and elements (energy, structure, patterns, findings, etc.) interact to explain or solve an issue or problem.

Process: To develop interpretation, analysis, and communication skills in the language arts, students will be able to:
- use evidence to develop inferences, justify arguments, and develop claims.

To understand ecosystems, students will be able to:
- create and interpret graphs related to population growth of living organisms; and
- analyze data related to the population growth of one species and its impact on the population of another species.

Concept: To develop conceptual thinking about interactions in the language arts and science, students will be able to:

- explain how interactions promote change in multiple contexts across multiple disciplines;
- synthesize information from various texts, sources, and models to support generalizations about interactions; and
- explain how interactions promote stability and change within an environment.

Accelerated CCSS for ELA

- RI.4.7
- W.4.2b
- W.4.2d
- SL.5.1d
- L.4.6

Accelerated NGSS

- 3-LS4-3
- 3-LS4-4
- 5-LS2-1

Materials

- Stopwatches (one per group of 3–4)
- Centimeter cubes or some type of counter (i.e., beans, pennies, etc.; several hundred for each group of 3–4)
- Sheet of paper with the numbers 20, 30, 40, 50, or 60 etc., written on it (one per group of 3–4)
- Videos:
  - "The War on Wild Pigs" (available at https://www.youtube.com/watch?v=W5YExLyblgQ)
  - "Feral Hogs in North America: An Overview" (available at https://www.youtube.com/watch?v=DadiycrLNP4)

- "History of Feral Swine in the Americas: Distribution of Feral Swine Over Time" maps (to display; available at https://www.aphis.usda.gov/aphis/ourfocus/wildlifedamage/operational-activities/feral-swine/sa-fs-history)
- Handout 1.5: Concept Organizer
- Handout 7.1: Boar Population and Plant Life
- Handout 7.2: Blank Science Analysis Wheel
- Rubric 1: Product Rubric (Appendix C)

Note: In this lesson, students will examine how the overpopulation of the wild boar impacts the environment. You may choose to read "Can Wild Pigs Ravaging the U.S. Be Stopped?" (available at https://www.scientificamerican.com/article/

can-wild-pigs-ravaging-the-u-s-be-stopped) or conduct an online search on the wild pig population in the U.S., so that you can provide context and background information to student discussions.

Introductory Activities

1. **Engage students in a quick debate:** Ask: *Should humans help control the growth or decline of animal populations?* Ask students to stand along a continuum that best supports their opinion. Solicit a variety of responses with their supporting evidence.
2. Explain that students are going to think about this question as they examine ways living things can become extinct or grow out of control.
3. Divide students into groups of 3–4, assigning one student the role of timekeeper, one the job of recorder, and another the job of population expert. (*Note*: When working in groups of four, the additional student can also be a population expert.) Each group will need a stopwatch, several hundred centimeter cubes or other things they can count (pennies, beans, counters, etc.), and a sheet of paper to keep track of their population's total.
   - Assign each group a different amount of time (20, 30, 40, 50 seconds) before their animal (centimeter cubes, beans, or other counters) population doubles.
   - Tell the class: *Your team is observing two animals in the wild over time. Your job is to keep track of how the population of that species grows. Every (20, 30, 40, 50, 60) seconds (depending on the number your group was assigned), the animals have babies, which means your population doubles. Keeping your stopwatch running, double your animal population on the given time interval and record how quickly your population grows in 3 minutes' time, assuming no animals die.*

4. Ask students to share their population sizes, and then discuss what surprised them about the population growth. (Sample response: It was hard to manage/keep track of the population because it was doubling so quickly; the more babies, the harder it was to control the population.)
5. Ask: *Why do some animals grow out of control while others stay in balance or become extinct?* Ask students to think about what they know about predators (those that hunt other animals) and prey (those that are hunted by other animals) to explain their answer. Ask: *What might the impact be on other plants and animals if the population continues to increase without any control?* (Students may mention the scarcity of resources, destruction of land, eating other animals that might be needed in a food web, or posing a threat to humans.)

6. Explain that students will explore interactions and balance within ecosystems in relation to animal populations. Students will be relying on math skills to help them explore population growth among real animal populations and the impact that uncontrolled growth of one species can have on ecosystems—especially when some species do not have as many predators.

In-Class Activities to Deepen Learning

1. Introduce the following real-life scenario that deals with imbalance in an ecosystem and the ways humans interacted to restore balance: Tell students you just got a letter from department of wildlife, and there is a problem with wild pigs: *The U.S. and the department of wildlife need your help and understanding of ecosystems to help with the following problem. Wild (feral) pigs and boars were first introduced to the United States when colonists began arriving from Europe about 400 years ago. Over the years, wild boars have been increasing in numbers, negatively impacting the environment. As the number of hunters declines each year and the growth of local populations requires a greater use of land, interactions among humans and wild boars has increased. Wild boar or "feral swine" populations have spread disease to other animal populations, impacted agriculture by tearing up the land, eating all of the vegetation that other animals and people rely on, and even damaged archaeological sites in different places across the U.S. They have few predators.*

    Note: There are many online videos from different department of wildlife institutions that explain the issue with wild boars across the U.S. that you could show instead of reading this scenario (see Materials list). It is likely that there is a video specific to your local area that you could find to show students, if desired. You could also have someone from your wildlife community agency discuss this issue or tailor it to another issue that is problematic in your area.

2. Show students the "History of Feral Swine in the Americas: Distribution of Feral Swine Over Time" maps (see Materials list). Ask:
    ▪ What do these graphics suggest about changes over time in the wild boar population?
    ▪ Why might this be of concern?
    ▪ Why do you think the population continues to grow?
    ▪ Why do you think their presence continues to spread throughout the U.S.?
    ▪ How might this impact the ecosystem?
    ▪ Why do you think wild boars are a bigger threat than other animals?

⬚ What questions would you want to have answered in ordered to figure out a solution to the problem? (Students may ask about lifespan, birthrates, food availability, or predators of pigs or lack thereof.)

3. Distribute Handout 7.1: Boar Population and Plant Life. Say: *As part of your task in collaboration with the department of wildlife, we need to estimate the number of pigs in a given area and figure out how their presence will impact the ecosystem. First, complete the final column in the table by determining the change in feral boar population year by year. (Annual population change is determined by subtracting those lost to starvation or hunting from the number of new offspring born each year.) After you have completed the table, construct a graph that shows how the population has changed. In the second part, you will compare the graph you have constructed for the boars to the graph already constructed (tuber population) to think about the boar's impact on the environment.*

Note: Data presented in both the table and the graph are fictitious, designed for this simulation only. However, the concepts derived are based in mathematical and ecologically relevant principles related to the problem. Allow students time to complete the handout in small groups. (Answers for right-hand column on Handout 7.1 are: +326, +461, +599, +1,065, +1,637, +2,224, +2,989, +5,157, +6,731, +11,270.)

4. Following the completion of Handout 7.1, discuss the following with your students. You do not need to ask every question and may assign different questions to small groups of students:

⬚ **Graph Questions:**
- ◆ What details do you notice in the graphs? What is a true statement you can make about the population of boars and availability of food?
- ◆ Why does the number of boars lost to starvation increase? What connections can you make to information learned in previous lessons regarding food chains/webs and ecosystems?
- ◆ What effect does the population growth have on the existing food web within the ecosystem according to the graphs?
- ◆ What do you notice about the growth of the boar population over time? Would increasing the number of boar hunters make a difference?
- ◆ What do you notice about how quickly the population grows/decreases based on the graph? Why does it increase or decrease?
- ◆ Create a label or caption for each graph that summarizes the message. What is your label, and how does your graph show that idea?

■ **Science Questions:**
  ◆ What does this graph assume about the boars included in the population? What does the graph assume about the growth and life cycle of the tubers?
  ◆ What additional information would we need in order to understand the devastation that might occur within the ecosystem?
  ◆ What are the short- and long-term consequences that the boar population increase would have on the food web and ecosystem they are a part of?
  ◆ What evidence suggests that humans should intervene and play a greater role in controlling animal populations? What additional information would you need to support your decision? What perspectives are missing?
  ◆ What new questions do you have that would help you make a responsible decision regarding the boar population?
  ◆ What are the reasons that some people might not want humans to intervene in animal populations?
  ◆ If a decision were made to increase the number of hunted boars per year, should hunters target male or female boars? Why does a decision like this matter? What consequences could this have on the ecosystem?
  ◆ What does the graph tell you about the severity of the problem (i.e., the potential for catastrophic ecosystem damage)?
  ◆ Based on the information you gathered, what would you tell the department of wildlife about the severity of the wild boar problem on the ecosystem? Why?

Science Analysis

1. Distribute Handout 7.2: Blank Science Analysis Wheel. Guide students through the following questions to analyze the scientific problem they are exploring. (See p. 207 of Appendix A for additional guidance on using the Science Analysis Wheel.) Refer students to the key question: *Should humans intervene to control the increase or decline of animal populations?* Next, explain that they are going to look at this problem for one species and issue only: wild boars. Add that students need not write complete answers, but that the Science Wheel is used as a guide for thinking about the issue.
  ■ **Real-World Issue or Problem:** *Should humans intervene to control the increase or decline of animal populations?*
  ■ **Center of the Wheel (Hypothesis):** *How does the wild boar population impact the ecosystem?*

Simple Science Questions:

- **Scientific Information:** What do you know about ecosystems that might help you answer this question?

- **Evidence/Data:** What do you predict might happen to the ecosystem if humans allowed the wild boar population to get out of control or decline? What do the data you collected with the graphing activity suggest? What new data might you collect to help you understand how big this problem is?

- **Findings/Solutions:** How might you model the different possibilities that could occur if humans intervened? If they didn't? What solutions might you consider if this problem continues?

- **Perspectives/Audience:** What perspectives are you considering as you think about this? What other perspectives need to be considered? (How might an animal activist examine this situation differently than a park ranger? How might a biologist and an ecologist examine this problem differently? Which perspective is most relevant to the real problem? Who else might need to examine or be impacted by this problem?)

- **Processes/Methods:** What steps might you consider in finding out an answer to determine the impact the boars are having?

- **Modeling:** How can you model the potential effects of this problem?

- **Cause and Effect:** What are the potential effects if humans don't intervene?

- **Stability and Change:** Are the changes that are occurring as a result of the increase or decline of the wild boar population positive, negative, or neutral?

- **Systems/Energy and Matter:** How does this affect the consumption and flow of energy within the ecosystem? How might this affect other living systems, such as animals or plants?

- **Patterns/Scale and Proportion:** Is the boar population contained, or might it increase and spread in negative ways if humans don't intervene? What patterns do you notice about animal movement or deaths (based on graphs, models, or experiments that have been conducted)?

- **Structure and Function:** What function does the boar serve in the environment? What about the plants the boars are eating?

Complex Science Questions:

- **Structure and Function + Systems/Energy and Matter:** How are the wild boar overpopulation and the flow of energy through the ecosystem related?

- **Cause and Effect + Perspectives/Audience:** How might an ecologist or biologist view the effects of the overpopulation of wild boars similarly or differently?
- **Findings/Solutions + Patterns/Scale and Proportion:** What solutions have others tried, and has this reduced the impact of the wild boars? What other solutions might work to reduce the overall impact of the wild boars on the plant life?
- **Scientific Information + Evidence/Data:** Who else has studied this, and how did his or her findings or solutions impact the questions you need to ask or answer? How might his or her evidence or data inform the new questions you need to study?
- **Stability and Change + Modeling:** How would you model the changes over time in the ongoing growth of the boar population without any human intervention? How do these models help us make decisions?

2. Say: *Remember that the U.S. and the department of wildlife needed your understanding of ecosystems to help with the overpopulation of boars. Now that you have a better understanding, what ideas would you offer? What solutions do you have? How might you use elements of the Science Analysis Wheel to test your solutions and determine whether or not they are possible?*

3. Ask students: *What impact does over- or underpopulation of species have on the ecosystem? Should humans intervene? How does your response differ or remain the same when considering the issue presented in* The Great Kapok Tree *versus the wild boar overpopulation?*

Choice-Based Differentiated Products

Students may choose one of the following (*Note:* Use Rubric 1: Product Rubric in Appendix C to assess student products):

- Think about what you have learned about producers, consumers, and decomposers within an ecosystem (from Lesson 2). Create a list of other living things that would be affected by the rapid growth of the boar population and the decrease of tubers. Design a model that shows the effects of the increase in boar population on other living organisms. How would it affect the balance among producers, decomposers, and consumers within a forest ecosystem? Be sure to include labels and a brief explanation.
- Would it be helpful to introduce a predator of wild boars into the ecosystem to solve this problem? Why or why not? Design a list of pros and cons, and then write three sentences that explain your response and reasons. Use parts of the Science Analysis Wheel to help you design your list and test your solution.

- Create a cartoon strip or skit that explains the need for balance within ecosystems and includes an example of how specific interactions between predators and prey can help maintain balance.
- Given what you learned in the previous lessons on food chains and webs, create a food web that includes the feral boars and the tubers. Include other animals and plants in the web that may be affected.

Opportunities for Talent Development

- Explore the concept of exponential growth by viewing an example that uses M&Ms as a model (see "Exponential Growth With M&M's" available at https://www.youtube.com/watch?v=qfYQUUC3F5I). Ask students to explore additional exponential scenarios and create their own scenario that includes exponential growth as related to a real-life problem.
- Ask students to research other invasive species within their community: *What other living organisms are affected by the species that are growing out of control? What solutions have been tried, and how did these work? What else can be done? Create a chart to show what has been done and whether or not it worked.*
- Is it ever okay to introduce a new animal into the environment? Have students explain the pros and cons of this idea by researching that animal and its potential benefits and problems in the environment. Students may present their findings to the class.
- Have students interview a local wildlife and game deputy in their community about issues they experience with maintaining the balance of ecosystems: *Generate at least 10 questions you could ask and have them approved by your teacher. After your interview, create a pamphlet or slogan that would help educate your community about the issues of overpopulation and ecosystem balance in your local area. Share it with the person you interviewed.*

Social-Emotional Connection

Use the following questions to lead students through a discussion: *What skills do you possess that would make you a good ecologist or a good mathematician? Which one of these jobs most appeals to you and why?*

ELA Task

Assign the following task as a performance-based assessment for this lesson: *Reflect in writing or discussion on the following prompt: How might overpopulation of species affect the living and nonliving things in the environment?*

Concept Connections

1. Add new information learned from this lesson to the generalizations about interactions on the class concept wall or to Handout 1.5 (continued from earlier lessons or see Appendix B).
2. Have students write a statement that includes at least two of the following words: *interactions, balance, ecosystems, overpopulation, predator, food.*

Assessment

▪ Assess student learning by examining choice-based differentiated products and rubric criteria, and/or Concept Connections reflections.

▪ Have students complete an exit ticket: *Explain or model the following question: Why are balanced interactions among populations of species within an ecosystem important?*

Handout 7.1

Boar Population and Plant Life

Directions: Your county recently participated in a national study that collected data related to feral boar population growth. The results of the data collected by your county are shown in the table below. You are tasked with determining the change in feral boar population based on the offspring, losses related to hunting, and starvation due to loss of vegetation within their habitat.

Part I

1. Complete the final column in the table by determining the change in feral boar population year by year.

Year	Feral Boar Population	Offspring	Starvation	Killed by Hunters	Feral Boar Population Change
2008	973	413	84	3	
2009	1,299	547	81	5	
2010	1,760	704	97	8	
2011	2,359	1,192	114	13	
2012	3,424	1,783	133	13	
2013	5,061	2,509	219	66	
2014	7,285	3,417	347	81	
2015	10,274	5,982	631	194	
2016	15,431	7,896	908	257	
2017	22,162	13,208	1,456	482	

Name: _____ Date: _____

2. Graph the *change* in feral boar population, using the chart you completed in Question 1.

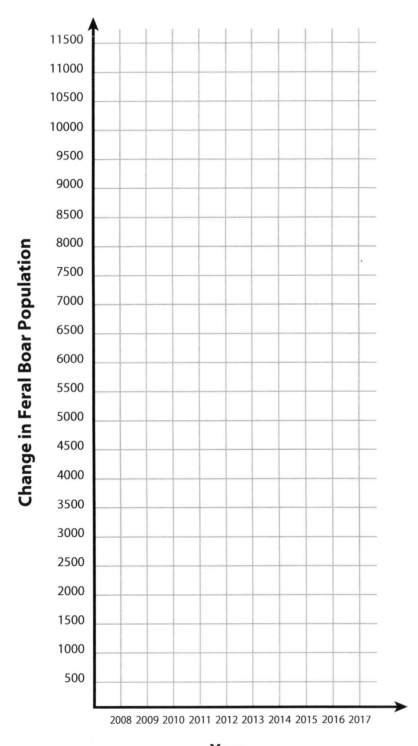

Year

Part II

Directions: The following graph shows the presence of a specific tuber plant that boars are known to eat and how many tubers are available over time. Compare the graph you have completed in Part I to the tuber graph listed here. What is the relationship between the tubers and the boar population over time? Write a sentence in the space at the bottom of this page to explain the relationship.

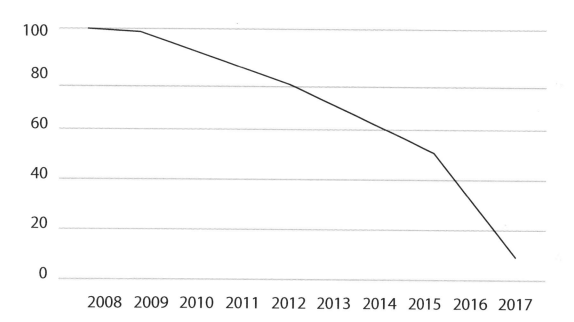

Percent of Tubers Available

Handout 7.2
Blank Science Analysis Wheel

Real-World Issue or Problem: _____

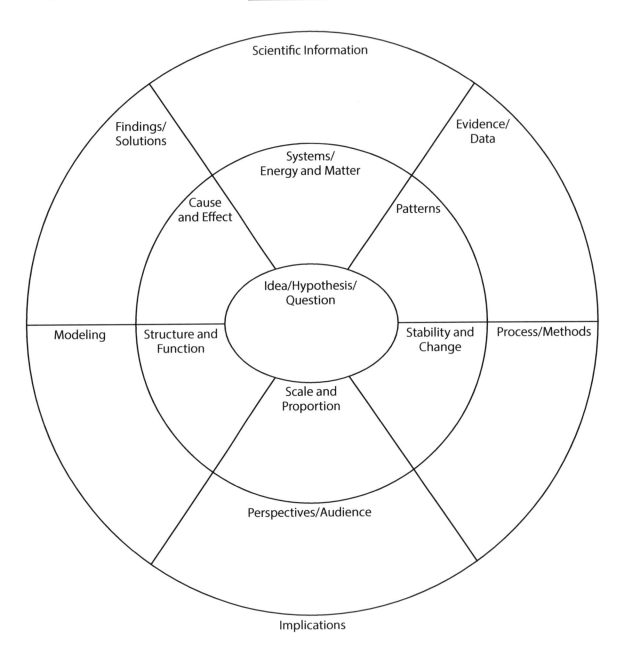

Created by Tamra Stambaugh, Ph.D., & Emily Mofield, Ed.D., 2017.
The middle section of the Science Analysis Wheel is adapted from the Next Generation Science Standards Crosscutting Concepts (National Research Council, 2012).

Lesson

8

Interactions Through Positive Relationships: Picture Book Study

Key Question

How can interactions help build positive relationships?

Objectives

Content: To analyze and interpret fiction, nonfiction, and art, students will be able to:

- analyze how literary elements interact to promote meaning within a story or poem;
- cite evidence in discussion and writing to support a point of view illuminated through literature, art, or nonfiction; and
- evaluate how an author uses language, structure, and point of view to reveal purpose and/or advance a claim.

Process: To develop interpretation, analysis, and communication skills in the language arts, students will be able to:

- respond to an analysis of literature, nonfiction, or art by developing arguments or elaborating on explanations through writing a variety of texts (e.g., essays and paragraphs, including relevant and sufficient evidence to support claims); and
- use evidence to develop inferences, justify arguments, and develop claims.

Concept: To develop conceptual thinking about interactions in the language arts and science, students will be able to:

- explain how interactions promote change in multiple contexts across multiple disciplines;
- synthesize information from various texts, sources, and models to support generalizations about interactions; and
- examine the relationship between interactions, relationships, and change in multiple contexts.

Accelerated CCSS for ELA

- RL.4.1
- RL.4.2
- RL.4.3
- RL.4.6
- RL.4.9
- RL.5.3

Materials

- Videos about positive interactions:
  - "Kid President - How to Change the World With Kindness" (available at https://ed.ted.com/on/iT4P09VO#review)
  - "Thousands of 'Buddy Benches' Help Thousands of Lonely Kids Find Friends" (available at https://www.nbcnews.com/nightly-news/video/-buddy-benches-help-thousands-of-lonely-kids-find-friends-947572291963)

- *The Other Side* by Jacqueline Woodson (optional read aloud available at https://www.youtube.com/watch?v=C80HdoDkHxY)
- *Each Kindness* by Jacqueline Woodson (optional read aloud available at https://www.youtube.com/watch?v=uSTbLZqGGSc)
- Handout 1.5: Concept Organizer
- Handout 8.1: Plot Interactions and Questions
- Handout 8.2: Blank Literary Analysis Wheel—Primary
- Rubric 1: Product Rubric (Appendix C)

Introductory Activities

1. Ask students: *How do interactions help us build positive relationships?* (Encourage students to think about their relationships with friends, family members, classmates, etc., and the ways that interactions help people connect with one another.)
2. View the two videos about positive interactions with students (see Materials list). As a group, discuss the videos using the following questions:
   - What does Kid President suggest about kindness?
   - What did Gabrielle hope to accomplish by adding a Buddy Bench to her school's playground? How do Buddy Benches help to promote positive interactions?
   - How do both Gabrielle and Kid President suggest that we use positive interactions to change the world around us?
   - Kid President says, "Things don't have to be the way they are. The world is changed by ordinary people." How can ordinary people change the world through their everyday interactions with one another?

In-Class Activities to Deepen Learning

1. Explain to students that they will be reading through two books by the author Jacqueline Woodson: *The Other Side* and *Each Kindness*. Students will be exploring how positive interactions, or a lack of positive interactions, can shape relationships.

2. In small groups or as a whole class, read through each story. (*Note*: A read aloud of each story is available in the materials section, or small groups of students may read their own copies of the books.)

3. Distribute Handout 8.1: Plot Interactions and Questions. Ask students to think about how the character interactions influence and bring about change within a story by completing the interactions plot map for each story. (*Note*: An example of the interactions plot map from the story *Jack and the Beanstalk* is provided in Figure 1 to give you an idea of how students might map positive and negative interactions in a story's sequence. It is important to note that the positive/negative slant of the interaction is often based on whether or not the interaction is being explored from the perspective of the protagonist or the antagonist.)

4. As a class, review the plot and interactions maps. Discuss the ways in which character interaction influenced turning points in the plot and how interactions and the development of character relations moved the story toward its resolution. Ask students to compare the two plot interaction maps: *How are the plot interaction maps the same or different? What does this say about the theme of the stories and the interactions of each plot?*

5. After discussing the plot interactions map, explore each of the two texts in more depth using the questions provided:

   ***The Other Side* by Jacqueline Woodson:**
   - **Sequence/Plot:** What is the sequence of events in this story?
   - **Structure and Style:** What word is repeated on the final page of the story? Why do you think the author chose to repeat that specific word? (Sample response: The repetition of "someday" is important, as the friends look to a future where "fences" do not divide people due to their differences.)
   - **Use of Words/Technique:** What does the fence symbolize in the story? (Sample response: It symbolizes a barrier, something separating the lives of both girls, segregation and racism, and the opportunity for friendship.)
   - **Feelings of the Author (Tone) and Reader (Mood):** How did you feel when Clover described Annie sitting or playing by the fence all alone? How did your feelings change when Clover and Annie first sit up on the fence together? (Students may say they are initially sad and then happy that the girls became friends.)

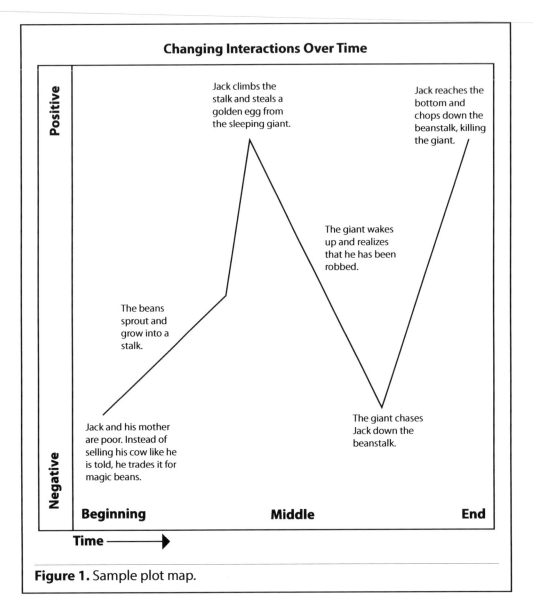

Figure 1. Sample plot map.

- **Setting:** When is this story set? Where do you think the story takes place? What inferences help you understand the setting? (Students may suggest that the story is set in the 1950s or 1960s in the American South based on the issue of segregation, the clothes that characters wear, and the way characters speak.)
- **Characters:** What are the commonalities between Clover and Annie? (Students may infer that the girls were both brave because they went against their parents' wishes/social norms at the time to play together.)

- **Point of View:** Why might the author have selected Clover's point of view for the story?
- **Conflict/Problem:** What social issue is addressed in this story? (Sample response: Segregation and the belief that people of certain races did not need to interact because, as Annie's mom says, "That's the way things have always been.")
- **Theme:** What is the theme of this story? (Sample response: Friendship is blind to color; just because things have always been done a certain way doesn't mean they are right; interactions can lead to positive changes, etc.)

Each Kindness **by Jacqueline Woodson:**
- **Sequence/Plot:** What is the sequence of events in this story?
- **Use of Words/Techniques:** What do Maya's hand-me-down clothes and simple toys symbolize in the story? (Sample response: Although they may symbolize poverty, they also stand out as things that are different from what Chloe and her friends are used to.)
- **Feelings of the Author (Tone) and Reader (Mood):** How did you feel when Maya attempted to interact with Chloe and her friends throughout the story? How did Chloe's feelings about herself change as a result of the demonstration with the pebble in class? (Students may feel disappointed or frustrated that Chloe is not willing to interact positively with Maya so she can have a friend. Chloe's feelings turn to regret when she realizes the impact that her actions could have had on Maya.)
- **Setting:** Describe the setting of the story. Why do you think the author chose the school setting for this story? (Sample response: The story takes place at school, a common setting, where students can sometimes behave in similar ways to Maya and Chloe. School is also a place students have access to regardless of how much money they have.)
- **Characters:** What inferences can you make about both girls based on their interactions with each other and their peers? (Sample response: Maya is a poor student who does not have many friends. She tries to befriend Chloe by sharing some of her simple toys with her. Chloe and her friends choose to ignore Maya's desire for friendship and instead make fun of her clothes and toys.)
- **Point of View:** How does the point of view of the narrator help us understand both girls better than if the point of view were of one of the girls?
- **Conflict/Problem:** What conflict is presented in this story? (Sample response: Chloe recognizes Maya's desire for friendship but does not respond with kindness.)

- **Theme:** What is the theme of this story? (Sample response: The theme is shared by Maya and Chloe's teacher when she says, "Each kindness makes the world a little bit better.")

Literary Analysis

Distribute Handout 8.2: Blank Literary Analysis Wheel—Primary. Tell students to consider the similarities and differences of *The Other Side* and *Each Kindness* as they answer the following questions. Consider using the cubes to ask questions about multiple elements (see Appendix A). The following questions may be used to lead discussion. Refer students to the plot interaction maps of each story as they answer questions, if needed.

1. **Feelings of Author (Tone) and Reader (Mood) + Use of Words/Techniques:** What is the mood at the end of each book, and how does the author use specific words to create images of happiness or sadness? Provide examples.
2. **Sequence/Plot + Theme:** How does the author use different plot structures to develop the same theme?
3. **Sequence/Plot + Characters:** What do Maya and Annie both want? How do their desires differ from those of Chloe and Clover? How do the different responses of each character influence the plot?
4. **Point of View + Feelings of Author (Tone) and Reader (Mood):** How does the difference in point of view (first vs. third) influence the mood (how the reader feels) of each story? Would a change in the point of view of either story change the mood? Why or why not?
5. **Conflict/Problem + Characters:** What are the similarities and differences in the conflict presented in each story? How does the conflict influence how the characters respond?
6. **Feelings of Author (Tone) and Reader (Mood) + Theme:** How does the author use opposite moods to develop a similar theme in each story?

Revisit the question asked at the beginning of the lesson (How do interactions help us build positive relationships?), and discuss how students' understanding of interactions and relationships has changed after viewing the videos and analyzing the two books by Jacqueline Woodson.

Choice-Based Differentiated Products

Students may choose one of the following to complete (*Note*: Use Rubric 1: Product Rubric in Appendix C to assess student products):

- Explore the connection between interactions, character relationships, and plot development using two different books or stories you know. Create a map like the one we created during the lesson that includes positive and negative interactions over the course of the book, using different colored pens or pencils to show both lines of development.

- Select another book you know, and create a cartoon strip that includes character interactions and the way characters' timing influences plot development, etc. Along with the visual representation, write a brief summary of the project that explains how one of the interaction generalizations influences emotion.

- Choose a story from today's lesson. Imagine you were to give advice or a gift to the main characters in the story (Clover and Annie, or Maya and Chloe) at three different parts of the interaction plot diagram. What advice or gift would you give them at each point and why? How would this interaction with the gift affect the characters' emotions, thoughts, or actions?

Opportunities for Talent Development

1. Ask students to consider a relevant problem within their community or school (e.g., bullying, loneliness, not enough parks, etc.): *Create an outline for a project (such as the buddy bench idea) that solves the problem in a positive way and does not require a lot of extra resources. How would this help build positive relationships within the community?*

2. Have students examine this video ("10 Kids That Changed the World," available at https://www.youtube.com/watch?v=m2CCPuOXJes) or others that show how kids have changed the world: *Write a letter to yourself about something you are passionate about and would like to do to create positive change.*

Social-Emotional Connection

Ask students to think about the positive and negative interactions between characters in the stories they read during this lesson: *How did the characters' emotions change before, during, and after the interactions? How did these characters deal with these emotions? Think about your own life. When you experience negative interactions with others, how do those emotions influence your actions or your relationships with others? What are some healthy ways to deal with unpleasant emotions? Create a mini-book that teaches others about healthy ways to deal with unpleasant emotions. Add your ideas and information from Woodson's books.*

ELA Task

Assign the following task as a performance-based assessment for this lesson: *Write a diary entry from the perspective of one of the characters in the story to show how her thoughts about _____ change because of her interaction with _____.*

Concept Connections

1. Add new information learned from this lesson to the generalizations about interactions on the class concept wall or to Handout 1.5 (continued from earlier lessons or see Appendix B). Consider making connections between emotions and the concept of power (power comes from a source, power can be used or abused, power is the ability to influence). What are the sources of power when interacting with others? How can power be used and abused within a relationship?

2. Have students write a statement that includes at least two of the following words: *interactions, relationships, life/lives, plot, characters, change, social, time.*

Assessment

- Assess student learning by examining choice-based differentiated products and rubric criteria, ELA Task responses, and/or Concept Connections reflections.
- Have students complete an exit ticket: *How do interactions among characters drive the plot of a story? Create a diagram or illustration and label it to explain your thinking.*

Handout 8.1
Plot Interactions and Questions

Part I

Directions: After reading the story, answer the following questions to help you think about interactions in the story and how the author uses different techniques to deliver a message.

1. Sequence the conflict events of the story using the following organizer to better understand the interactions. You may draw or write your ideas.

What is the problem or conflict in the story?

What happens first to explain the problem? (First)

How do different characters attempt to solve the problem? (Next)

What is the solution? How is it resolved? (Finally)

2. How does the setting help establish our understanding of the characters?

3. How does the conflict build your understanding of the theme? What do the characters learn from the conflict? How does that help us understand the theme?

4. What figurative language do you notice (similies or metaphors, for example) in the story? How does it help you understand the story better?

5. How does the narrator's point of view influence the message or theme?

6. How do character interactions lead to changes in their relationships? In the way you feel as a reader?

Part II

Directions: Complete the interactions map, noting the positive and negative inter-actions that occur over time, and answer the questions that follow. Think about the chart you completed in Part I, Question 1, as you create this interactions map.

Changing Interactions Over Time

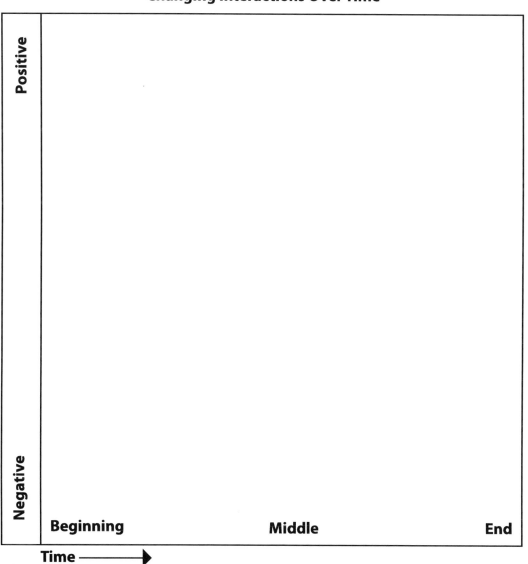

Name: _____ Date: _____

1. How do interactions among the main characters lead to changes in their emotions? How do interactions it affect their lives?

2. When did the interactions become more positive or negative? How or where is this reflected in the plot map?

3. What impact did the interactions have on the characters' relationships over time?

4. What role did the interactions and relationships of the characters have on your understanding of the theme?

Name: _____ Date: _____

Handout 8.2

Blank Literary Analysis Wheel—Primary

Directions: Draw arrows across elements to show connections.

Text: _____

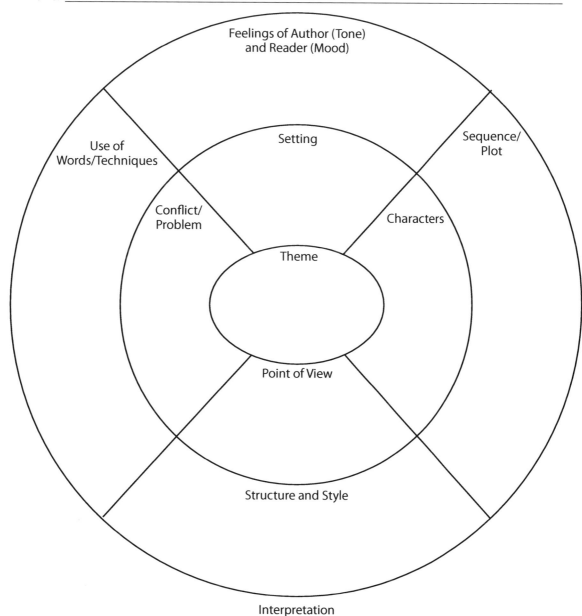

Created by Tamra Stambaugh, Ph.D., & Emily Mofield, Ed.D., 2017.

Lesson

9

Interactions and Change: The True Story of Ivan

Key Question

Should animals be kept outside of their natural habitats?

Objectives

Content: To analyze and interpret fiction, nonfiction, and art, students will be able to:

- analyze how literary elements interact to promote meaning within a story or poem;
- cite evidence in discussion and writing to support a point of view or main idea illuminated through literature, art, or nonfiction; and
- evaluate how an author uses language, structure, and point of view to reveal purpose and/or advance a claim.

To understand ecosystems, students will be able to:

- explain and demonstrate how natural and manmade changes in ecosystems lead to positive or negative changes for living organisms; and
- analyze how scientific elements (energy, structure, patterns, findings, solutions, etc.) interact to explain or solve an issue or problem.

Process: To develop interpretation, analysis, and communication skills in the language arts, students will be able to:

- use evidence to develop inferences, justify arguments, and develop claims.

To apply knowledge of ecosystems, students will be able to:

- compare and contrast how animals behave before and after changes within their ecosystems or habitats; and
- debate the implications and consequences of keeping animals in captivity.

Concept: To develop conceptual thinking about interactions in the language arts and science, students will be able to:

- explain how interactions promote change in multiple contexts across multiple disciplines;
- synthesize information from various texts, sources, and models to support generalizations about interactions; and
- examine the relationship between interactions, relationships, and change in multiple contexts.

Accelerated CCSS for ELA

- RL.4.1
- RL.4.2
- RL.4.3
- RL.4.7
- RL.5.3
- RI.4.2
- W.4.1b
- W.4.1c
- W.4.2d
- SL.5.2
- SL.5.3

Accelerated NGSS

- 3-LS3-2

Materials

- *Ivan: The Remarkable True Story of the Shopping Mall Gorilla* by Katherine Applegate (teacher's copy for read aloud or one copy per groups of 3–4)
- Videos about zoos:
    - "Why Do We Need the Modern Zoo?" (available at https://www.youtube.com/watch?v=XOrPmOXhxo0)
    - "The Pros & Cons of Zoos" (available at https://www.youtube.com/watch?v=RHBuAOp5upU)

- Handout 1.5: Concept Organizer
- Handout 9.1: Pros and Cons Analysis
- Handout 9.2: Blank Literary Analysis Wheel—Primary
- Rubric 1: Product Rubric (Appendix C)

Introductory Activities

1. Ask students: *Should animals be kept in zoos?* Students may stand in a circle and take turns saying either "Yes, because . . . " or "No, because. . . . " They may also agree or disagree with others' ideas. Explain that students will be looking at how animals respond to changes in their environment. Make sure

the students have read *The One and Only Ivan*, as this lesson is the true story of Ivan's life and will give away the end of the novel.

2. Distribute Handout 9.1: Pros and Cons Analysis. As students view the videos about zoos (see Materials list), encourage them to listen for the points and supporting evidence that are presented for both sides of the debate. Turn on the captions for "The Pros & Cons of Zoos" video, as the information is presented at a fairly quick pace.

3. Divide students into groups of 3 or 4. Ask them to share their pro and con arguments from their recording sheets. Share responses with the class.

Read Text

Explain that students are going to be reading the true story of Ivan, a gorilla who was kept in captivity, in *Ivan: The Remarkable True Story of the Shopping Mall Gorilla*. Distribute copies of the book to small groups of 3–4 students to read (if available; teachers may also read aloud or check online for a read aloud if needed). Tell students that as they/you read, they should be thinking about how animals respond when introduced to a different ecosystem. They should also be listening for interactions among literary elements in the text.

Distribute Handout 9.2: Blank Literary Analysis Wheel—Primary or Literary Analysis Cubes to ask questions about multiple elements (see Appendix A).

Simple Questions:
1. **Sequence/Plot:** What events led to Ivan's release?
2. **Theme:** How does your knowledge about ecosystems help you better understand the message or theme of the true story of Ivan? What lesson or big idea does the author want you to take away from reading this?
3. **Characters:** What were the positive and negative character interactions in Ivan's life?
4. **Setting:** What are the main settings for the story? How do they compare to the natural ecosystem in which Ivan is supposed to belong?
5. **Feelings of Author (Tone) and Reader (Mood):** How do you feel as a result of reading about the true story of Ivan? Why?
6. **Feelings of Author (Tone) and Reader (Mood):** How do you think the author feels about Ivan's circumstance? How do you know?

More Complex Questions:
1. **Setting + Characters:** How do Ivan and the people around him change as the setting changes?
2. **Use of Words/Techniques + Theme:** If you were to create a symbol for the true story of Ivan that captured the theme of his life, what would your symbol be? Why?

3. **Sequence/Plot + Characters:** How do the changes in Ivan's environment over time (from the beginning, middle and end of the story) affect his well-being?
4. **Feelings of Author (Tone) and Reader (Mood) + Setting:** How does the setting in which Ivan lives for most of his life create the mood (reader's feelings) of the story?
5. **Feelings of Author (Tone) and Reader (Mood) + Use of Words/Techniques:** What language or words does the author use to set the tone (author's feelings) of the story?

In-Class Activities to Deepen Learning

1. Revisit the question: *Should animals be kept in zoos?* Ask students to find a partner and create a skit in which Katherine Applegate and Mack from the Big Top Mall talk about whether or not animals should be kept in captivity. Remind students to stay true to character and use the information from the story or the video to support their conversation. (If you need to divide students into groups of three due to the size of the class, the third person can be the interviewer and moderate the conversation.)
2. After students have had some time to create their skits, allow a few groups to share. Discuss their ideas.
3. Remind students of the science connection by sharing the following NGSS Disciplinary Core Idea (LS2.C): "When the environment changes in ways that affect a place's physical characteristics, temperature, or availability of resources, some organisms survive and reproduce, others move to new locations, yet others move into the transformed environment, and some die" (National Research Council, 2012). Provide students with blank pieces of paper, and ask them to create a diagram that shows how this is evidenced using Ivan's real-life story and how he responded to the changes in his environment. Include the impact of biotic and abiotic factors.

Choice-Based Differentiated Products

Students may choose one of the following to complete (*Note*: Use Rubric 1: Product Rubric in Appendix C to assess student products):

- Explore some of the major differences that exist between the novel and the real-life story of Ivan. Students can sequence the events in both *The One and Only Ivan* and *Ivan: The Remarkable True Story of the Shopping Mall Gorilla*. Consider the following questions: Why do you think the author chose to change Ivan's story in the novel? What impact did the additional interactions (Stella, Ruby, Mack, George, Julia, etc.) have on Ivan within the novel?

- Bring in or list eight objects that represent Ivan's attributes, the theme, and important parts of the sequence of events within his life as listed in the true story of his life. Include a written description of what each item represents. Be abstract rather than literal (e.g., a crumpled piece of paper represents Ivan's habitat). Present this to the class.
- Create a Venn diagram that compares and contrasts how settings in stories and settings in animal habitats positively and negatively impact the characters or species.
- Create a brochure for a new zoo opening soon. Include some ways it addresses some of the arguments against zoos. Include how it strives to promote "mutually beneficial" interactions between humans and animals, as well as specifically how it strives for positive interactions between the animal and environment.

Opportunities for Talent Development

- Have students learn about the life of Koko the gorilla (video available at https://www.youtube.com/watch?v=sesspfZKsq0), who spent more than 40 years learning sign language while living in captivity. Ask students to compare the lives of Ivan and Koko, exploring their interactions with humans and ways in which animals change due to interactions within changing environments. (*Note*: This activity may require additional assistance from teachers in terms of resources, as students may wish to learn more about Koko. The idea is that students make a connection between the way animal interactions change as a result of their changing environments. Koko learned sign language and Ivan painted, things that they learned to do only as a result of changed environments and additional interactions.)
- Have students examine a zoo habitat in their area: *Critique that habitat, and provide compliments and suggestions for redesign based on what you see and know about animal ecosystems and captivity. Write a letter that includes your findings and encourages the staff to build animal enclosures that mirror animals' natural environment. Include information about how changes in environment lead to changes in interactions, which can be both positive and negative. Provide examples from the life of Ivan as well as what you know about ecosystems.*

Social-Emotional Connection

Ask students to share about times when they visited a zoo either as part of a class field trip or with family and friends. How do they feel as a result? Why? Explain that emotions propel us to "move" (e-*motion*) and are there for a reason. Ask: *What does your experience at the zoo "move" you to do or think about?*

ELA Task

Assign the following task as a performance-based assessment for this lesson: *Complete the following paragraph by developing sentences that use evidence from the book and videos: Animals can be kept in zoos under certain conditions. It is appropriate for animals to be kept in zoos if. . . .*

Concept Connections

1. Use Handout 1.5: Concept Organizer (continued from earlier lessons or see Appendix B) to guide students to understand how the ideas of interactions presented in this lesson relate to the interactions generalizations. In the last row, students may consider how interactions relate to the concept of *change* and its generalizations (change happens over time, change is inevitable, change can be positive or negative, change can be manmade or natural, and change can be orderly or random).

2. Interactions allow for changes. Have students explain three changes experienced by animals when they are in zoos, using evidence from the book and videos.

3. Revisit the class concept generalization map. Ask students to make connections between this lesson and other ideas from previous lessons. Use arrows and words to illustrate relationships.

Assessment

- Assess student learning by examining choice-based differentiated products and rubric criteria, ELA Task responses, and/or Concept Connections reflections.
- Have students complete an exit ticket: *How do changes in environment lead to changes in interactions that are both positive and negative?*

Handout 9.1
Pros and Cons Analysis

Directions: Complete the chart about the pros and cons of keeping animals in zoos. As you watch the videos, listen for the points and supporting evidence that are presented for both sides of the debate.

Pros: Animals should be kept in zoos.	Cons: Animals should not be kept in zoos.
Point 1: Evidence:	Point 1: Evidence:
Point 2: Evidence:	Point 2: Evidence:

Handout 9.1, Continued

Pros: Animals should be kept in zoos.	Cons: Animals should not be kept in zoos.
Point 3: Evidence:	Point 3: Evidence:
Questions I Still Have:	

Interactions in Ecology and Literature © Prufrock Press Inc.

Handout 9.2

Blank Literary Analysis Wheel—Primary

Directions: Draw arrows across elements to show connections.

Text: _____

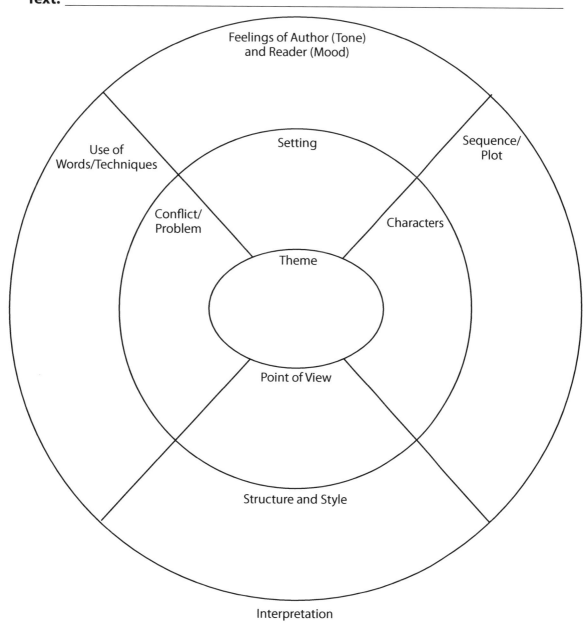

Created by Tamra Stambaugh, Ph.D., & Emily Mofield, Ed.D., 2017.

Lesson

10

Interactions and Teamwork

Key Question

How do group interactions help others survive?

Objectives

Content: To analyze and interpret fiction, nonfiction, and art, students will be able to:

- cite evidence in discussion and writing to support a point of view illuminated through literature, art, or nonfiction.

Process: To develop interpretation, analysis, and communication skills in the language arts, students will be able to:

- respond to an analysis of literature, nonfiction, or art by developing arguments or elaborate on explanations through writing a variety of texts (e.g., essays, paragraphs, including relevant and sufficient evidence to support claims), and
- use evidence from a variety of sources to create an argument.

To apply knowledge of ecology, students will be able to:

- provide a persuasive argument that animals work in groups to survive.

Concept: To develop conceptual thinking about interactions in the language arts and science, students will be able to:

- explain how interactions promote change in multiple contexts across multiple disciplines;
- synthesize information from various texts, sources, and models to support generalizations about interactions; and
- examine the relationship between interactions, relationships, and change in multiple contexts.

Accelerated CCSS for ELA

- W.4.2b
- W.4.2d
- W.4.3d
- W.4.9
- L.4.6

Accelerated NGSS

- 3-LS2-1

Materials

- Videos:
  - "Funny Animation: How Animals Work in Team" (available at https://www.youtube.com/watch?v=kWhZRahpgXE)
  - "Study Jams – Symbiosis" (available at https://www.youtube.com/watch?v=0UHMUIGhGNg)
  - "Exploring Ecosystems: Coral Reef Symbiosis | California Academy of Sciences" (available at https://www.youtube.com/watch?v=-EUUEPinEcQ)
  - "Whales Team Up in Amazing Bubble-Net Hunt | National Geographic" (available at https://www.youtube.com/watch?v=z00G0RxeSP0)
  - "Ingenious Bubble Net Fishing – Nature's Great Events – BBC" (available at https://www.youtube.com/watch?v=Q8iDcLTD9wQ)

- Chart paper and markers
- Handout 10.1: Animal Behavior Cards
- Handout 10.2: Literary Interactions and Symbiosis Characteristics
- Science Analysis Wheel (Appendix B)
- Rubric 1 (Appendix C)

Introductory Activities

1. Divide students into groups, and assign each group one of the following phrases. Discuss the meaning of each phrase with a real-life example:
   - Birds of a feather flock together.
   - One is greater than two.
   - Big fish eat little fish.
   - Out of sight, out of mind.
   - Two heads are better than one.
   - The whole is greater than the sum of its parts.
   - If you want to go fast, go alone. If you want to go far, go together.

2. Ask: *How might these popular sayings apply to animal populations? What about human populations?*

3. Next, tell students they are going to play "amoeba tag." Set ground rules and monitor safety. (*Note*: There are many versions of the game found online, such as this one: http://www.ultimatecampresource.com/site/camp-activity/amoeba-tag.html.) To play, two people are "it." They hold hands and chase people. Any person they catch joins the chain by linking hands. When another person is caught, the chain can stay together or split two and two. The chain must split into even numbers, but it can link back together at will. This game is played until everyone is connected to the chain.

4. Afterward, ask: *What does this game suggest about teamwork? What skills did you need in order to tag others? What worked? What didn't? How did the size of the group impact your effectiveness? What does this game say about interactions?* (Connect to interaction generalizations.)

5. Show the video "Funny Animation - How Animals Work in Team." Ask: *What does this video show about teamwork and animals? What was their primary purpose for working together?* (Students may note that the animals needed to work in groups to protect themselves.)

In-Class Activities to Deepen Learning

1. Explain to students that they are going to look at ways animals interact in groups and why.

2. Ask students which animals they can think of that work in groups. They may mention bees, ants, wolves, etc. Ask: *Why might animals work in groups?* Solicit a variety of responses. Guide students to understand that animals work in groups to defend themselves, hunt for food, and adjust to changes.

3. Divide students into groups, and assign each group one of the animal cards from Handout 10.1. After reading the passage, tell students they are to answer at least two of the following questions with their group and draw a model for each to show their thinking. (*Note*: These questions are developed from the Science Analysis Wheel. It is not necessary for students to write on the wheel to answer these questions, although you may want to guide student thinking by referring to it as a visual).

   ▪ **Problem +Systems/Energy and Matter:** From the perspective of your animal group, what are the problems they face? How do the interactions within the group help address these problems?

   ▪ **Proportion and Cause-Effect:** What would happen if your group size were cut in half? What impact would this have on your group community and on your survival?

- **Structure and Function + Stability and Change:** After reading your section, how is your "group community" organized? What are the main parts and how do they relate to each other? How does this structure allow for stability and balance?
- **Findings/Solutions + Stability and Change:** What inferences can you make about the way your animal community handles changes in their environment?
- **Scientific Concepts + Systems/Energy and Matter:** How does what you know about food webs, ecosystems, abiotic factors, and biotic factors help you understand how your animal group interacts?

4. Then, distribute chart paper and markers for each group. Explain that groups are to read about their specific animal and create a "wanted" poster or job description for their animal that outlines the characteristics needed for working in a group and includes how the animal's role in a group allows for defense, hunting for food, and/or adjusting to changes in the environment. (Revisit Lesson 2 if more information on food chains is needed.)

Note: If students are interested in seeing examples of how animals work in groups, there are numerous video clips online that show examples of animals working in groups, such as bubble netting of humpback whales (see Materials list) or meerkats watching out for predators. Preview videos ahead of time if you choose to show any examples, as some of the videos can be quite graphic and upsetting to students.

5. Ask students to discuss in groups the following questions:
   - *Not all animals live in groups. What are some examples of solitary animals?* (Students may mention snakes, bears, butterflies, polar bears, skunks, leopards, koalas, rhinos, turtles, pandas, tigers, frogs, etc.)
   - *Why do only some animals live in groups but not others?* (There are no definitive answers regarding this. It could be that some animals do not live in groups because of the amount of food they need to eat—the competition for resources would be too great if they were in a group. Others do not need to help finding food because they can get the resources available on their own. Others need larger spaces to survive and thrive without other individuals like them in their territory. Some animals may even appear to live in groups only because it is convenient or there is a lot of food, but they do not interact. For example, bears who are mostly solitary as adults may eat from berry bushes in close proximity, or birds may all roost in the same mountain for shelter, as it is the only place available and safe.)

For animals, what are the benefits and liabilities of living in groups versus living alone? (Students may note that group living can cause scarcity of food, competition for mates, additional protection, support with raising and protecting young, help finding food, competition for the food that is found, etc.)

6. Explain that not only do groups of the same animals work together, but different species may also rely on each other in different ways. These are called *symbiotic relationships*. Explain that "sym" means together or with, and "bio" means life, so a symbiotic relationship is the interaction or working together of living things. There are three types: parasitism, mutualism, and commensalism.

7. Show the videos about symbiosis ("Study Jams - Symbiosis" and "Exploring Ecosystems: Coral Reef Symbiosis | California Academy of Sciences"; see Materials list). Ask students to examine the types of relationships among different species in the ecosystem.

8. Afterward, discuss the following questions:
    - What are the differences between parasitism, mutualism, and commensalism? (Parasitism is a positive/negative relationship, where one species benefits and one is harmed; mutualism is a positive/positive relationship, where both species benefit; and commensalism is a relationship where one species benefits and the other is not affected.)
    - How do symbiotic relationships support an ecosystem? (Students may discuss how animals rely on each other or interact with each other in positive, negative, and mutually beneficial ways to survive.)
    - Which interaction generalizations are most evident in symbiotic relationships? (Answers will vary; refer to the interaction generalizations.)
    - Do all ecosystems, regardless of where they are located, act in predictable ways? (Students may note that the coral reef and the forest—as with all other biomes—have similar patterns of interactions, but the animals that live there are different.)

9. Tell students to think about group interactions among characters in the books they read or situations you have discussed in this unit. Ask students to complete Handout 10.2 individually or in small groups by assessing the type of interaction for each pairing in Column 1 and providing an example. There are empty rows for students to add additional pairs or for teachers to assign.

10. Upon completion of the charts, ask students to share their ideas and examples, coming to a consensus about areas of disagreement. (*Note*: Students may have examples in various columns for the same character pairs—especially if the characters changed throughout the course of the story.) Ask:

How are interactions among characters in a book like an ecosystem? (Students should note interactions and relationships among living things that affect each other. They may also mention how different pieces of the story and character development rely on each other, and one affects the other.)

Choice-Based Differentiated Products

Students may choose one of the following to complete (*Note*: Use Rubric 1: Product Rubric in Appendix C to assess student products):

- In the video on coral reef symbiosis, you saw how marine biologists and ecologists study ocean life and their interactions and create charts and graphs to make predictions about the future health of the marine ecosystem. Design an outline for a study you would like to conduct about animal interactions in your environment. Use the Science Analysis Wheel (Appendix B) to think through your ideas. Write down questions and ideas in each part of the wheel as a way to help you plan.
- Create a short skit (no more than 2 minutes) that shows the differences between parasitism, commensalism, and mutualism and teaches at least two different interaction generalizations.
- Create a fable that demonstrates the moral "teamwork makes the dream work." In your fable, include animals as characters and explain scientifically valid principles about how your chosen animal species works in a group for survival. Include thoughts your characters may have and dialogue between them to help the reader understand your animal group interactions.

Opportunities for Talent Development

- Have you ever heard of a flock of birds? A pride of lions? Animal groups have names. Have students research different animal group names and create an alliterated book or game with an answer key to teach others what different animal groups are called: *Develop at least 12 different group names. For example, what is a group of hippos called? What about a group of cats . . . a group of crocodiles . . . a group of zebras?*
- What is an anthropologist? Jane Goodall was a famous anthropologist who studied chimpanzees and learned more about their world and how they interact. (See p. 205 for a biography of Jane Goodall that can be shared with students.) Have students read more about her: *Research what she liked to do growing up and how that led her to become an anthropologist, including what she contributed to the world of anthropology. If you were to be an anthropologist, what would you study? What questions would you want to know more about?*

Social-Emotional Connection

Ask students: *Do you work best in a group or alone? Why? When working in groups, what strengths do you bring to a group? What would the principles of parasitism, commensalism, and mutualism look like in group work? When you disagree with others, especially when working with a group, what are ways in which you can move toward "mutualism" (a win-win) in your interactions with others? Make a list of strategies.*

ELA Task

Assign the following task as a performance-based assessment for this lesson: *Write a paragraph to convince others about how some animals work in groups to obtain food, adjust to changes, and/or defend themselves. Provide examples from different animal groups.*

Concept Connections

1. Add new information learned from this lesson to the generalizations about interactions on the class concept wall or to Handout 1.5.
2. Have students write a statement that includes at least two of the following words: *interactions, survival, parasitism, mutualism, groups, commensalism, food, hunt, animals.*

Assessment

- Assess student learning by examining choice-based differentiated products and rubric criteria, ELA Task responses, and/or Concept Connections reflections.
- Ask students to complete the following exit ticket: *How are interactions among characters in a story and animals groups similar and different?*

Handout 10.1
Animal Behavior Cards

MEERKATS

Meerkats are small mammals that are members of the mongoose family. They are the only members of the mongoose family that do not have bushy tails. They use their strong tails to help them balance when they are standing up. These squirrel-sized animals live in deserts and grasslands in Southern Africa. Meerkats live in burrows that they dig with their claws. Their claws are long and strong, which make them good for digging. They have a special membrane over their eyes that protect them as they dig.

These cute and furry animals are very social and live in groups of up to 40 that are called "mobs," "gangs," or "clans." Because meerkats live primarily underground, they can stay safe from predators. Their burrows are as deep as 15 feet and have different entrances, tunnels, and rooms. Meerkats sleep in their burrows, but as the sun rises, they emerge and look for food. As some meerkats search for food, others stand guard watching out for predators. If the meerkat on guard sees a predator, it loudly barks to warn the others. They have different barks and whistles for different types of threats. Meerkats have good eyesight and sense of smell, which guides them in looking for spiders, caterpillars, scorpions, and the other small critters that they eat.

As some meerkats are hunting and looking out for predators, others stay behind in the burrow and care for the meerkat pups. Different meerkat mobs can be rivals and try to kill each other's young. Meerkats also create safe places in their hunting areas called *bolt-holes*. They hide in these holes if a large predator, such as an eagle or hawk, tries to attack. If the meerkats are found by their predators out in the open, they stand together and hiss at their predator. Sometimes meerkats are able to trick their predators into thinking they are one large animal. If meerkats are caught alone, they lie on their backs and try to look fierce by showing their teeth and claws. Meerkats can run about 20 miles per hour, which they sometimes have to do to escape their predators. Despite being threatened by predators, their average lifespan is 7–10 years in the wild and 12–14 years in captivity, and they are not an endangered species.

References

National Geographic Kids. (2017). *Meerkat*. Retrieved from https://kids.nationalgeographic.com/animals/meerkat/#meerkat-group.jpg

Science Kids. (2016). *Fun meerkat facts for kids*. Retrieved from http://www.sciencekids.co.nz/sciencefacts/animals/meerkat.html

Your Kid's Planet. (2015). *Meerkat facts for kids*. Retrieved from http://yourkidsplanet.com/meerkat-facts-for-kids

Handout 10.1, Continued

LIONS

Lions live in Sub-Saharan African grasslands, scrub, and open woodlands. They are the second largest cats in the world, only smaller than tigers. Lions live in prides, groups of about 10–30 lions. Prides are made up of three males, 12 related females, and their young. Prides are bigger when there is more food and water available, and smaller when these resources are low. Lions' roars can be heard up to 5 miles away and are used to keep track of each other. The male lions guard the large territory and the lion cubs. The territories can be as large as 100 square miles. When the male lions are protecting their territory, they may get in fights with other animals. Male lions' thick manes help protect their necks when they fight.

Female lions do not have thick manes. Females hunt for their pride. Because they are smaller than the males, they are faster. Lion are fast, but their prey is usually faster. Lions have to rely on teamwork to bring their prey down. The smaller female lions form a semicircle around the prey and herd the prey toward the center. The stronger female lions make the kill. Hunting typically happens at night. Lions have many prey, including antelopes, buffalos, zebras, young elephants, crocodiles, and giraffes.

When lions have successful hunts, they share their food with their pride. Adult males get first dibs on the food, then the female lions, and finally the cubs. Lions will drink water every day if it is available. If it is not available, lions can survive for 4–5 days without drinking water. Lions are very lazy animals, and they spend 16–20 hours of the day sleeping or resting. They usually sleep in trees and groom one another as they rest. When lionesses give birth, they usually have 2–3 cubs. The cubs are raised together by all of the females in the pride. In the wild, lions live up to 16 years. In captivity, they can live up to 25 years. Lion cubs are hunted by hyenas, leopards, and jackals. Lions are at risk for extinction because of loss of habitat and being hunted by humans.

References

Active Wild. (2015). *Facts about lions for kids*. Retrieved from https://www.activewild.com/facts-lions-kids
Animal Fact Guide. (2014). *Lion*. Retrieved from http://www.animalfactguide.com/animal-facts/lion
Morgan, E. (n.d.). 10 lion facts! *National Geographic Kids*. Retrieved from https://www.natgeokids.com/au/discover/animals/general-animals/10-lion-facts/

WHALES

There are approximately 80 different species of whales that come in all different shapes and sizes. Whales are warm-blooded and live in groups to take care of their babies and make sure that everyone gets food. The groups are often made up of all males or all females. Whales breathe air through their blowhole, which also spits out water.

Humpback whales are 40-ton mammals and are the noisiest type of whales. Male humpbacks can "sing" for up to 15 minutes at a time, and the noise travels across large distances. Their sounds are believed to be communication with others and a way to attract potential mates. Humpback whales live near coastlines and eat small fish. To capture these fish, they use a strategy called bubble netting. In this hunting practice, the humpback whales use their blowholes to herd and contain fish. They migrate every year to areas near the equator as a way to keep warm. Mothers stay close to their young, and when they swim together, their flippers often touch. Female humpbacks nurse their babies for almost a year. Humpbacks live in pods of 2–15 whales. Humpbacks are strong swimmers, and their large tails help propel them through the water.

Another type of whale, Orca whales, hunt larger animals such as walruses, seals, penguins, sea turtles, and even sharks. Orca whales are enormous animals and eat about 500 pounds of food every day. Orcas hunt in pods made up of family members. They herd fish into a small area so that they are easier to hunt. Orca whales can slap their tails on the surface of the ocean to make a giant wave that pushes penguins and sea lions into the water. To hunt seals, they bump them off the ice. Orcas may even hunt blue whales. As a pod, they circle around large prey. Orcas can swim about 30 miles per hour and are slightly shorter in length than a school bus.

References

Brill. (2011). How humpback whales catch prey with bubble nets. *ScienceDaily*. Retrieved from https://www.sciencedaily.com/releases/2011/06/110624083516.htm

National Geographic Kids. (n.d.). *Humpback whale facts!* Retrieved from https://www.natgeokids.com/nz/discover/animals/sea-life/humpback-song

National Geographic Kids. (2017). *Orca*. Retrieved from https://kids.nationalgeographic.com/animals/orca/#orca-jumping.jpg

Science Kids. (2016). *Fun whale facts for kids*. Retrieved from http://www.sciencekids.co.nz/sciencefacts/animals/whale.html

ZEBRAS

Recognized for their black and white stripes, no two zebras look exactly the same. The stripes on zebras help protect them from predators. When zebras are in groups, their appearances make them difficult to single out. Predators are not always able to go after one single zebra. Zebras are members of the horse family, and there are several different types of zebras. Like horses, zebras gallop and trot, but they are not as fast as horses. Also like horses, zebras sleep standing up.

Different species of zebras have different types of stripes. Zebras are grazing animals that use their sharp front teeth to bite grass and then chew it with their duller back teeth. Zebras move around a lot as they look for fresh grass and water. As they migrate, they sometimes gather in herds of thousands of zebras. These mammals sometimes travel with other grazers such as wildebeests. Like some other mammals, zebras groom one another. What appears to be biting each other is actually pulling loose hairs off each other.

Zebras live in grasslands in Africa and can live for 25 years. They can run up to 35 miles per hour, which they often need to, in order to escape predators such as lions. The lead zebra sounds an alarm call when danger is spotted. If a herd is being chased, they often zigzag from side to side, so they are more difficult to catch. Zebras can run for long distances, which helps them run from predators. Baby zebras stay with their mothers for at least one year, and they can easily recognize their mother's stripe pattern. Baby zebras can walk right after being born and can run within an hour of being born. This is helpful for escaping predators. Zebras have great eyesight, even at night. Their night vision is similar to an owl's. Their eyes are located on the sides of their heads. Zebras also have excellent sense of smell and taste.

References

Active Wild. (2015). *Zebra facts for kids*. Retrieved from https://www.activewild.com/zebra-facts-for-kids

KidsKonnect. (2008). *Zebra facts*. Retrieved from https://kidskonnect.com/animals/zebra

National Geographic Kids. (2017). *Zebra*. Retrieved from https://kids.nationalgeographic.com/animals/zebra/#zebra-herd.jpg

Name: _____   Date: _____

ELEPHANTS

Elephants are the largest land mammals and have one of the longest lifespans of many large mammals in their habitat. Elephants live for 50–70 years in the wild. They weight up to 6.6 tons. In the wild, elephants live in families called herds, made up of female elephants. The only males that live in herds are the calves, and they stay in the herd until they are about 15 years old. After a male leaves the herd, he often lives alone. The elephant that's in charge of these herds is called the matriarch, and she is the usually the oldest elephant. In their herds, new mothers are helped by the other adult females. These helping females are called "aunties" and are chosen by a new mother. Because elephants only give birth every 5 years, raising their young is very important to their survival.

Elephants are herbivores and only eat plants, grass, and fruit. Elephants are very smart and can peel their own bananas. They love to swim and play in the water, and they drink a lot of water as well. Adult elephants may drink up to 60 gallons of water every day. Elephants suck the water into their trunk and spray it into their mouths. Elephants also use their trunk to spray themselves like a shower. African and Asian elephants have different trunks. At the bottom of Asian elephants' trunks, they have one "finger." The bottom of African elephants' trunks has two "fingers." Elephants are very protective of their trunks because they are sensitive and used to breathe, drink, pick up food, smell, touch, and communicate. Their trunks are used to caringly touch a loved one and are used in self-defense. Elephants are emotional creatures and cry when they are upset. Elephants also squeak and trumpet when they are happy. Just like humans, elephants grieve for the dead.

These large mammals have great memories and are so smart that they are able to play jokes on humans. Male and female elephants have large tusks that continue to grow throughout their life. Tusks are used for digging, foraging (searching for food), and fighting. Sometimes elephants use their tusks to rest their heavy trunks. Elephants can make many different sounds, but they mostly communicate through low-frequency sounds. Elephants can judge the distance from another elephant based on how the noise sounds. Even though elephants are extremely large, they only need 3–4 hours of sleep per day.

References

Animal Fact Guide. (2014). *African elephant.* Retrieved from http://www.animalfactguide.com/animal-facts/african-elephant

EleAid. (2017). *Elefacts.* Retrieved from http://www.eleaid.com/eleaiders/elefacts

Guenther, T. (2017. *Elephants: Facts.* Retrieved from http://www.kidzone.ws/animal-facts/elephants/facts.htm

Name: _____ Date: _____

CHIMPANZEES

Chimpanzees are social animals and similar to humans in many ways. Chimp and human DNA is 98.5% the same. Chimpanzees have fingers and toes and expressive faces, and they hug to show love. They learn skills, such as finding safe food to eat, by observing their mothers and other adults. Chimps are omnivores, so they eat plants and meat. They enjoy ripe fruit the most, but they also like leaves, flowers, bird eggs, and insects. Chimpanzees live in groups from 15 to 80 members led by a strong alpha male. They travel, sleep, and find food in these groups. Members of these communities come and go very frequently, so there are often new community members. Females give birth every 5–6 years, usually to one chimp at a time. Occasionally chimps give birth to twins. In their first months of life, baby chimps hang on to their mother's belly and travel everywhere with her. After a few months, chimps spend the next 7–10 years near their mothers and observe their grooming, nesting, and hunting behavior. They also groom each other to remove dirt and bugs. Grooming helps keep them clean and also helps build friendships between chimps. Like humans, chimpanzees know how to use tools. They often use rocks to crack open nuts and use sticks to get insects out of nests and logs. Chimps typically walk on all fours, but they can also stand and walk upright on two legs. Another way that chimpanzees get around is by swinging from branch to branch. These smart creatures do most of their eating and sleeping in trees. Chimpanzees live in tropical forests and woodland savannas in Africa. They are an endangered species and live up to 45 years in the wild. The biggest threat to chimpanzees is loss of habitat. To communicate, chimps use different gestures, facial expressions, grunts, and screams.

References

Defenders of Wildlife. (n.d.). *Chimpanzee: Pan troglodytes*. Retrieved from http://www.kidsplanet.org/factsheets/chimpanzee.html

National Geographic Kids. (2017). *Chimpanzee*. Retrieved from https://kids.nationalgeographic.com/animals/chimpanzee/#chimpanzee-with-baby.jpg

ANTS

Ants are insects with six legs. They live in many different habitats. There are more than 12,000 species of ants in the world. Each species is a little bit different from each other. Ants live in large colonies or groups. Some colonies have millions of ants. The three different types of ants that live in colonies are: the queen, the female workers, and the males. The queen and the males have wings. The queen is the only ant that can lay eggs. Once the queen is an adult, she spends all of her life laying eggs. She also sleeps much more than other ants. Some colonies have one queen, and other colonies have many queens. The role of the male is to mate with the queen. Some of the ants protect the queen and defend the colony. Other ants gather or kill food, and attack enemy colonies. If they successfully attack another colony, they take their eggs. Another role of ants in a colony is to take care of the eggs and babies. One type of ant is called the Argentine ant. They eat nearly anything. When they are looking for food, they leave trails everywhere they go. This helps them make sure they do not look in the same area twice.

One type of ant, the Argentine ant, builds nests in wood. They can damage houses and buildings. Carpenter ants do not eat the wood that they remove. They eat plant nectar, dead insects, meat, and sugary food. Another type of ant is the Odorous house ant. They give off a rotten smell if they are crushed, which is why they are called "odorous." This type of ant lives in houses and can contaminate food by leaving waste behind. The Bullet ant lives in the Amazon and has an extremely painful sting. Fire ants also can be harmful, but they bite rather than sting. Ants are very small, but incredibly strong. An ant can carry 50 times its own body weight. Ants often work together to move bigger objects. Ants live on every continent on earth, except Antarctica. Ants don't have ears, and some don't have eyes either. To "hear," they listen to vibrations from the ground with their feet. The largest ant nest ever found was more than 3,700 miles wide in Argentina, and billions of ants lived inside.

References

antARK. (2017). *Amazing ant facts*. Retrieved from http://antark.net/ant-facts

National Geographic Kids. (n.d.) *10 cool facts about ants!* Retrieved from https://www.natgeokids.com/nz/discover/animals/insects/ant-facts

Pest World for Kids. (2014). *Ants*. Retrieved from http://pestworldforkids.org/pest-guide/ants

Name: _____ Date: _____

BEES

Bees are flying insects that usually have yellow and black stripes on their backs. There are almost 20,000 different species of bees. They live in many different habitats on every continent except Antarctica. Bees have a very good sense of smell. They can tell different flowers apart based on the smell. Bees fly from flower to flower and sip on the nectar of the plant. Bees have a tongue that is really good at sucking up nectar. They store the nectar in their throat until they get back to the hive. At the hive, the nectar is turned into honey to use as food. When bees land on flowers, they collect pollen. Bees have fuzzy bodies that help them collect pollen. They spread this pollen around to reproduce the flowers.

Honeybees and bumblebees live in colonies or hives. Hives have up to 40,000 bees. Each bee has a special job. Newly hatched bees clean up around the hive. Worker bees build the honeycomb, take care of the eggs, and collect food. Queen bees lay eggs. Male drone bees mate with the queen bee. Worker bees have to visit 4,000 flowers to make one tablespoon of honey. Gathering nectar and pollen can be dangerous, because big spiders and bugs hide in flowers to capture the bees. Queen bees have to lay thousands of eggs every day to make sure they do not go extinct. When a queen bee dies, workers raise a new queen. They pick a young bee and feed her "royal jelly." This special food helps the young bee develop into a queen that can lay eggs. Some bees have stingers. If bees think that their hive is in danger, they may try to sting. Female worker bees sting the most frequently. Queen bees do not sting very often. Male drone bees do not have stingers. Honeybees die after stinging. Honeybees are also very fast flyers. They beat their wings 200 times every second. They can also fly about 15 miles per hour. Bees do a special dance called their "waggle dance." This dance tells the other bees where to find the best food.

References

KidsKonnect. (2007). *Bee facts*. Retrieved from https://kidskonnect.com/animals/bee

National Geographic Kids. (n.d.). *10 facts about honey bees!* Retrieved from https://www.natgeokids.com/za/discover/animals/insects/honey-bees

San Diego Zoo Kids. (2017). *Arthropod: Bee*. Retrieved from http://adminkids.sandiegozoo.org/animals/insects/bee

Wonderopolis. (2017). *Why do bees sting?* Retrieved from https://wonderopolis.org/wonder/why-do-bees-sting

Handout 10.2
Literary Interactions and Symbiosis Characteristics

Directions: Think about the characters or situations from this unit and their interactions. Which interaction from the column headings best describes the relationship? Are there other interactions that might also be true? What evidence do you have?

Select which interaction best describes the relationship. Then, provide an example in the appropriate column. An example and a few character or situation pairs have been added for you. Add other examples in the empty rows. Compare your ideas with a partner or small group. Where did you disagree? How can you come to a consensus?

	One Benefits and One Is Harmed	Both Benefit in Different Ways	One Benefits but the Other Is Unaffected
Ivan and Mac (From *The One and Only Ivan*)	*Mac benefits from receiving money as people visit Ivan; Ivan is harmed because he is caged and unhappy. He has no one to protect.*		
Ivan and Ruby (From *The One and Only Ivan*)		*Ruby is able to learn from Ivan, and Ivan has someone to protect.*	

Name: _____ Date: _____

	One Benefits and One Is Harmed	Both Benefit in Different Ways	One Benefits but the Other Is Unaffected
Clover and Annie (From *The Other Side*)			
Wild Boars and Plants			

Lesson

11

Interactions Within Us: Biography Study

Key Question

How do a person's interactions with his or her life experiences impact his or her future?

Objectives

Content: To analyze and interpret fiction, nonfiction, and art, students will be able to:

- cite evidence in discussion and writing to support a point of view or main idea illuminated through literature, art, or nonfiction.

Process: To develop interpretation, analysis, and communication skills in the language arts, students will be able to:

- respond to an analysis of literature, nonfiction, or art by developing arguments or elaborating on explanations through writing a variety of texts (e.g., essays and paragraphs, including relevant and sufficient evidence to support claims); and
- use evidence to develop inferences, justify arguments, and develop claims.

Concept: To develop conceptual thinking about interactions in the language arts and science, students will be able to:

- explain how interactions promote change in multiple contexts across multiple disciplines;
- synthesize information from various texts, sources, and models to support generalizations about interactions; and
- examine the relationship between interactions, relationships, and change in multiple contexts.

Accelerated CCSS for ELA

- RL.4.1
- RI.4.1
- RI.4.9
- RI.5.3
- RI.5.9
- W.4.9

Materials

- Videos:
  - "Famous Failures" (available at https://www.youtube.com/watch?v=zLYECIjmnQs)
  - "Zootopia – Train Scene (Try Everything)" (available at https://www.youtube.com/watch?v=Pj75bnsCM_k)
  - "'Get Back Up Again' Clip | Trolls" (available at https://www.youtube.com/watch?v=IFuFm0m2wj0)

- Handout 1.5: Concept Organizer
- Handout 11.1: Failure and Success Quotes
- Handout 11.2: Biographies
- Handout 11.3: Interaction of Failure and Success Matrix
- Rubric 1: Product Rubric (Appendix C)

Introductory Activities

1. Distribute Handout 11.1: Failure and Success Quotes. Divide students into groups of 3–4. Students should paraphrase and interpret selected quotes and draw an illustration to represent the meaning of the quote (some groups may be assigned more than one quote). Consider providing students with background information about the individual each quote is attributed to.

2. Ask students to share their quotes and illustrations. Share the video "Famous Failures" (see Materials list). Ask: What did all of these individuals have in common? How did they respond to situations that they faced? What can we learn about the interaction between failure and success from them?

3. As a class, develop generalizations about failure and success that students believe to always be true. (Sample responses: Failure is an important part of success; you have to work hard after you fail in order to succeed; you have to learn from your mistakes in order to be successful when trying something new; etc.)

In-Class Activities to Deepen Learning

1. Students will be listening to two songs from well-known animated movies (*Trolls* and *Zootopia*; see Materials list). If possible, ask a student to briefly summarize the plot and describe some of the problems or failures that the main character (Poppy or Lt. Judy Hopps) faces throughout the story. Listen to the songs with students. If possible, provide captions, so students can follow along with the words as they listen to the message of the song.

2. Discuss the messages presented in each song (themes relating to failure and persistence), and ask the following questions:
   - How did each character interact with/respond to failure or hardships as he or she encountered them?
   - How do the characters' interactions with failure make them smarter, stronger, or ready to face the next challenge?
   - How can failure influence a person's ability to interact with others or interact with his or her work toward a specific goal?

3. Distribute Handout 11.2: Biographies and Handout 11.3: Interaction of Failure and Success Matrix to students. Students will read through each of the biographies and use the matrix to organize examples of the individuals' failure and success. Then, ask students to describe the interaction between failure and success in that individual's life and make a connection to an interaction generalization. Finally, have students draw a symbol that represents that individual's failure/success story. (*Note*: It may be beneficial to work through one of the biographies and the individual's row on the matrix together as a class so students can develop an understanding of the pattern they should be following. Figure 2 is an example.)

4. Revisit the earlier generalizations made by the class. Discuss whether or not they would keep those generalizations or add new ones based on what they read. Ask: *How did the individuals interact with the failures that they faced? How did their interactions with others (publishers, coaches, critics, etc.) influence the way that they handled failure and used it to become successful?*

Choice-Based Differentiated Products

Students may choose one of the following to complete (*Note*: Use Rubric 1: Product Rubric in Appendix C to assess student products):
   - Once you have completed the matrix for J. K. Rowling, Michael Jordan, and Walt Disney, think about one or two fictional or animated characters of your choosing (e.g., one of the main characters from the animated videos used earlier in the lesson). Complete a similar matrix for those characters.

	Failures and Struggles	Successes	Interaction Between Failure and Success	Connection to a Generalization	Symbol
J. K. Rowling	A single mother who lived on welfare; her book was initially rejected by publishers.	Published the Harry Potter series (seven books) that would go on to become bestsellers around the world. Her books have since been turned into movies, video games, and amusement parks.	One of the publishers told her, "Don't quit your day job." She used that rejection to go back and spend more time making her first book even better.	Interactions are inevitable: Her mother's death (interaction with grief/loss) inspired her as a writer and influenced her characterization of Harry Potter (who also lost his parents in the first book).	Lightning Bolt: Symbolic not only of the Harry Potter series, but also of the fact that lightning bolts interact with the environment and cause change.

Figure 2. Sample interaction of failure and success matrix.

Then, create a visual representation (Prezi, PowerPoint, diorama, etc.) of your characters' failures, struggles, and the interaction between two.

- Select one of the three individuals that you learned about in this lesson (J. K. Rowling, Michael Jordan, and Walt Disney). Given what you know, choose a "theme song" that could be connected with that character. What song connects to their experiences with failure and success? What theme song would they walk out to if they were speaking at your school? Once you have chosen a song, write a brief summary as to why that song fits the individual based on their experiences and interactions with failure and their eventual success.

Opportunities for Talent Development

- Ask students to interview someone older than them: *Ask about his or her successes and failures and what he or she learned. How do his or her ideas about successes and failures compare to the biographies of famous people he or she has read? What advice would you give this person for success based on his or her response?*

- Have students select a famous person they respect and read his or her biography or find out more about his or her life through an online search: *What personal characteristics made him or her strong? How did he or she view or interact with his or her life experiences in a way that helped him or her be successful? Create an acrostic poem using his or her name, listing the personal attributes and attitudes he or she had toward success and failure as the letters of his or her name.*

Social-Emotional Connection

Discuss failure, defeat, and the effect that interactions with others have on our success. Have students reflect back on a time when they have failed when trying something new, such as riding a bike or playing a musical instrument. Ask: *How did you feel when you faced failure or defeat? Did you want to get back up and try again right away? Did another person (a parent, coach, friend, teacher, etc.) step in and provide words of encouragement? How do our interactions with others influence the way we handle failures?*

Concept Connections

1. Use Handout 1:5: Concept Organizer (continued from earlier lessons or see Appendix B) to guide students to understand how the idea of interactions presented in this lesson relates to the interactions generalizations. Consider asking students to make connections with choice (choosing to interact with failure in a positive way) as a source of power.
2. Revisit the class concept generalization map. Ask students to make connections between this lesson and other ideas from previous lessons. Use arrows and words to illustrate relationships.

Assessment

- Assess student learning by examining choice-based differentiated products and rubric criteria, ELA Task responses, and/or Concept Connections reflections.
- Have students complete an exit ticket: *Is there a right way to interact with failure? What lessons can we learn from other famous people who have experienced failure that help us understand our actions and ourselves?*

Handout 11.1
Failure and Success Quotes

Directions: Select, paraphrase, and interpret a selected quote. Then, draw an illustration to represent the meaning of the quote on the back of this handout or on a separate sheet of paper.

"Success is not final; failure is not fatal: it is the courage to continue that counts."
>—Winston Churchill (Former Prime Minister)

"There are no secrets to success. It is the result of preparation, hard work, and learning from failure."
>—Colin Powell (Former Secretary of State)

"Think like a queen. A queen is not afraid to fail. Failure is another stepping-stone to greatness."
>—Oprah Winfrey (talk show host, actress, and businesswoman)

"Failure is simply the opportunity to begin again, this time more intelligently."
>—Henry Ford (Founder, Ford Motor Company)

"I can accept failure; everyone fails at something. But I can't accept not trying."
>—Michael Jordan (basketball player and businessman)

"You build on failure. You use it as a stepping stone. Close the door to the past. You don't try to forget the mistakes, but you don't dwell on it. You don't let it have any of your energy, or any of your time, or any of your space."
>—Johnny Cash (country music singer-songwriter)

"The greatest glory in living lies not in never failing, but in rising every time we fall."
—Ralph Waldo Emerson (19th-century poet and philosopher)

"It is impossible to live without failing at something, unless you live so cautiously that you might as well not have lived at all, in which case you have failed by default."
—J. K. Rowling (author of the Harry Potter series)

"Winning is great, sure, but if you are going to do something in life, the secret is learning how to lose. Nobody goes undefeated all the time. If you pick up after a crushing defeat, and go on to win again, you are going to be a champion someday."
—Wilma Rudolph (Olympic sprinting champion)

"My greatest concern is not whether you have failed, but whether you are content with your failure."
—Abraham Lincoln (Former President)

"Success and failure are both part of life. Both are not permanent."
—Shah Rukh Khan (actor)

Handout 11.2
Biographies

J. K. ROWLING

"It is impossible to live without failing at something, unless you live so cautiously that you might as well not have lived at all, in which case you have failed by default."

—J. K. Rowling

Born in 1965 to parents of simple means, Joanne Rowling, who went by Jo, grew up in England and Wales. She began writing at the age of 6, and by the time she was 11 had completed her first novel. After graduating from Exeter University in 1987, she worked a variety of jobs, none of them relating to writing. In 1990, Rowling's mother passed away from Multiple sclerosis, a disease that affects the nervous system. As a result of her sadness and grief, she moved to Portugal where she took a job teaching English. While there, she met the journalist who would become her husband, and together, they had a daughter together. Her marriage was not a happy one, and it ended in divorce after only a year. Following her divorce, she and her daughter moved to Scotland in 1995 to make a new start. Rowling struggled to support herself and her daughter, relying on welfare. Although they were not homeless, Rowling's inability to find work made it so she and her daughter struggled financially. It was during this time that Rowling found herself struggling with depression. To combat her unhappiness, she turned back to her love of writing, choosing to revisit a book idea that came to her years before.

The idea to write a book about a young wizard first came to Rowling while riding a train to London one day in 1990. She would spend years developing the characters and the plot of the entire Harry Potter series before starting in on the first novel, *Harry Potter and the Philosopher's Stone*. After receiving the manuscript of the first book, Rowling's literary agent worked hard at finding a publishing company who would be willing to print and promote the book. Publishers were hesitant, with one even telling her to keep her day job. Rowling and her agent pushed through the rejection letters until finally, in 1997, Bloomsbury Children's Books published the first novel of the series. It was a smashing success in the United Kingdom and was soon published in the United States and countries all over the world. In the years that followed, six more books were added to the Harry Potter series. In total, the Harry Potter series has been translated into more than 30 languages, with millions of copies sold worldwide.

Rowling and her creation of the world of Harry Potter had such a profound impact on the lives of readers across the world that she would go on to receive multiple awards and honors, including the Order of the British Empire (2001), a prestigious medal awarded to individuals who make significant contributions to the United Kingdom. From sales of books and licensing rights, Rowling has become one of the wealthiest women not only in the United Kingdom, but also the world. Following the success of Harry Potter in literature, film, and amusement parks, Rowling founded her own charitable organization, Lumos, that supports more than 8 million children worldwide who live in institutions due to poverty, a disability, or displacement (homelessness). In 2008, Rowling was invited to give the commencement speech at the Meeting of the Harvard Alumni Association. During her speech, she reflected on the hardships she had faced in her life: poverty, divorce, and rejection. Her love of writing and her persistence over failure, however, helped her find success in life.

References

Biography.com (2017). *J. K. Rowling.* Retrieved from https://www.biography.com/people/jk-rowling-40998

J. K. Rowling. (2016). *J. K. Rowling* .Retrieved from https://www.jkrowling.com

Lumos. (n.d.). *About.* Retrieved from https://wearelumos.org/about

Rowling, J. K. (2008). The fringe benefits of failure, and the importance of imagination. *Harvard Magazine.* Retrieved from https://harvardmagazine.com/2008/06/the-fringe-benefits-failure-the-importance-imagination

MICHAEL JORDAN

"I can accept failure; everyone fails at something. But I can't accept not trying."

—Michael Jordan

Imagine turning out to play your favorite sport, only to be cut from the team. Would you believe that this happened to one of the greatest athletes of all time? Despite the fact that he is now recognized as one of the greatest basketball players in the history of the game, Michael Jordan failed to make the varsity team in high school. Jordan would go on to use his experience being cut from the team as a source of motivation to improve his skills.

Although he was born in Brooklyn, NY, in 1963, Michael Jordan grew up in North Carolina. After his experience in high school, Jordan worked hard and focused on mastering his technical skills. He attended the University of North Carolina at Chapel Hill and quickly stood out as the team's strongest player. Before starting his senior year of college, Jordan was drafted into the National Basketball Association in 1984 by the Chicago Bulls. During that same summer, he played on the U.S. basketball team at the Olympic Games in Los Angeles, CA. Averaging 17 points a game, Jordan helped the team win the gold medal. Professionally, Jordan continued to amaze and was selected for the All-Star Game and named Rookie Player of the Year. At times, teammates who had been playing for longer than Jordan felt as though he was getting too much attention. However, Jordan continued to impress them with his leadership on and off the court.

Jordan would continue to play for the Chicago Bulls through 1998 and then go on to serve as both a partial owner and then player for the Washington Wizards. During the 1990s, Jordan took a break from basketball and joined the Birmingham Barons minor league baseball team as an outfielder, proving himself to be a multisport athlete. All told, Jordan played professional basketball for 15 seasons, winning six NBA Championships (1991–1993 and 1996–1998). A recipient of numerous awards and recognitions, Jordan has been inducted into the NBA Hall of fame twice, once for his own accomplishments and another time for "The Dream Team," the name given to the U.S. basketball team that won gold at the 1992 Olympics.

Outside of his athleticism and contributions to the popularity of basketball as a global sport, Jordan worked hard to create a number of successful businesses. Throughout his career and into his retirement, Jordan was paid to be a spokesperson for a number of large companies, including Nike, Coca-Cola, McDonald's, and many more. Jordan even has his own line of shoes with Nike, Air Jordans. In 1996, while still playing basketball for the Chicago Bulls, Jordan starred in the live-action/animated movie *Space Jam*, which made more than $200 million. Due to money made playing basketball, endorsements, ownership in various sports teams, and business deals, Jordan became the first NBA player to be valued at more than $1 billion. In 2016, President Barack Obama honored Michael Jordan with the Presidential Medal of Freedom, the highest award given to citizens who make important cultural contributions.

Michael Jordan is a name that most will recognize, if not for his athletic ability then for the many commercials he appeared in and the celebrity status that he holds. However, his humble beginnings and his failure to make the high school basketball team suggest that he was the type of person who was not willing to accept failure. Instead, he used that failure as an opportunity, one that motivated him to become one of the greatest American athletes ever known.

References

Biography. (2017). *Michael Jordan.* Retrieved from https://www.biography.com/people/michael-jordan-9358066

NBA.com Staff. (2017). *Legends profile: Michael Jordan.* Retrieved from http://www.nba.com/history/legends/profiles/michael-jordan

Newsweek Special Edition. (2015). Michael Jordan didn't make varsity—at first. *Newsweek.* Retrieved from http://www.newsweek.com/missing-cut-382954

WALT DISNEY

"Everyone falls down. Getting up is how you learn to walk."

—Walt Disney

The rise in popularity of animated films would not have been possible without the genius of Walter Elias Disney, more commonly known as Walt Disney. Born in Illinois in 1901, Disney grew up sketching and drawing. By the time he was in high school, he was contributing cartoons to the school newspaper and taking drawing and photography classes at the Chicago Art Institute in the evenings. By the age of 17, Disney dropped out of school and moved to Missouri to pursue his dream of being a professional cartoon artist. He was fired from the first newspaper he worked for. His failure did not set him back. Disney continued to experiment with cel animation, a process where some parts of a picture or "frame" are used repeatedly in an animated scene. With a partner, Disney started his own company and began producing short animations of fairy tales. The company, called Laugh-O-Gram Studio, did not have enough money to stay in business and declared bankruptcy in 1923.

Following his initial failure as a cartoon artist and businessman, Disney moved to Hollywood, CA, to start a new company with his brother. Their first project together was on a series of short films based on a fantasy novel written in 1865, *Alice's Adventures in Wonderland*. Disney's first character creation was "Oswald the Lucky Rabbit," but he lost the animation rights to a film producer named Charles Mintz. However, Disney persisted with his animated creations and soon developed a character named Mickey Mouse in 1928. Producers at another studio told him Mickey Mouse would terrify women and never work. Thankfully, the success of Mickey worked for Disney, and, following a series of successful short animations, he went on to introduce notable characters, such as Donald Duck, Goofy, Pluto, and Minnie Mouse, in the years that followed. Disney and his team worked hard to develop their animation techniques and, by 1937, released *Snow White and the Seven Dwarfs*. The film would go on to bring in an initial $1.5 million in revenue and win eight Academy Awards. Following their newfound success, Disney and his brother Roy moved their parents into a home near their studios. Less than a month later, their mother Flora died from a furnace complication. This loss left Walt with a great deal of sadness, as he not only grieved his mother's passing, but also felt somewhat guilty for allowing her to live in a home with a broken furnace.

Throughout the 1950s and 1960s, many of the classic animated films, such as *Pinocchio*, *Peter Pan*, and *101 Dalmatians*, were produced by Walt Disney's studio. Through the films his studio produced, Disney received 22 Academy Awards, more than anyone else in history. Beyond producing animated films, Disney dreamed of creating a theme park where families could come and see the animated worlds they enjoyed come to life. Thanks to his studio's financial success, Walt purchased a 160-acre orange grove and opened Disneyland in 1954. The theme park increased in popularity very quickly, with families from all over the United States, and eventually the world, spending time with some of their favorite movie characters. Eventually, Disney parks opened in major cities all across the world, which today include Orlando, Paris, Shanghai, Hong Kong, and Tokyo.

Disney died at the age of 65 from complications related to lung cancer. The studio that he built from the ground up with his brother continues to operate theme parks, create movies, and entertain families across the world. Despite being fired as a cartoonist, going bankrupt, and losing his mother, Disney persisted to create a company that is recognized by people in practically every country.

References

Biography. (2017) *Walt Disney*. Retrieved from https://www.biography.com/people/walt-disney-9275533

JustDisney.com. (n.d.). *Walt Disney, biography*. Retrieved from http://www.justdisney.com/walt_disney/biography/long_bio.html

Walt Disney Parks and Resorts. (n.d.). *Destinations around the world*. Retrieved from https://aboutdisneyparks.com/about/around-the-world

Handout 11.3

Interaction of Failure and Success Matrix

Directions: Read each biography on Handout 11.2. Then, use the matrix to organize examples of the individuals' failure and success.

	Failures and Struggles	Successes	Interaction Between Failure and Success	Connection to a Generalization	Symbol
J. K. Rowling					
Michael Jordan					
Walt Disney					

Lesson

12

Culminating Project

Key Question

What role do interactions play in ecosystems and literature?

Objectives

Choose specific unit objectives as they relate to each product option (see pp. 13–15).

Materials

- Handout 1.5: Concept Organizer (completed from previous lessons or see Appendix B)
- Handout 12.1: Culminating Project
- Rubric 2: Culminating Project Rubric (Appendix C)

Discussion

Remind students about the concept generalizations explored in this unit. They may revisit Handout 1.5: Concept Organizer or the class concept map:

- Interactions are inevitable.
- Interactions allow for changes.
- Interactions are caused by multiple influences.
- Interactions can be positive, negative, or mutually beneficial.

Ask: *How do some of the lessons connect? What patterns do you notice? Are there any new generalizations we can make about interactions?*

Student Reflection

Ask students to reflect on their learning throughout the unit:

1. What have you learned about yourself as a learner? What new information have you learned about ecosystems? About interactions with story elements? Are there any new fields of study you are interested in? What new questions do you have?

2. Consider how interactions generalizations cross multiple subjects and are present even in our own lives. Provide a personal example for each generalization. Create a chart, similar to Handout 1.5: Concept Organizer, but use your own real-life examples, as well as examples from other subject areas (math, social studies, physical education, etc.), instead of the specific examples shared throughout this unit.

3. What is the relationship between interactions in science, literature, and art? How are these the same and different? Create a symbol that illustrates the connection between them. Explain in 1–2 paragraphs why your symbol for interactions is appropriate, using the information you have learned in this unit.

Choice-Based Differentiated Products

1. Assign the culminating project (Handout 12.1). Students may choose based on their interests. At teacher discretion, students can present parts of the project to the class.

2. Use Rubric 2: Culminating Project Rubric (Appendix C) to assess student products.

ELA Practice Task

Assign the following task as a culminating performance-based assessment: *Why are interactions important in ecosystems and literature? After reading the texts, analyzing art, and learning about science concepts in this unit, write at least three paragraphs to answer the question. Refer to at least three lesson ideas to develop your response and cite specific evidence from the works.*

Name: _____ Date: _____

Handout 12.1
Culminating Project

Directions: Choose one product choice to demonstrate your understanding of what you have learned throughout this unit.

1. Write a story that incorporates similar themes to that of *The Great Kapok Tree*, *The One and Only Ivan*, etc. Before writing, preplan by thinking through the elements on the Literary Analysis Wheel—Primary. Think about a real-world problem that you will address in your story, specifically how your fiction story reveals the implications of interactions between humans and nature. Consider how setting will affect the characters and problem. Consider how the interactions affect characters as you develop your story. Include elements of figurative language, symbolism, and dialogue.

2. What unanswered questions did you have throughout this unit? Choose a question and explore the topic or issue further. What are the different points of view about the topic, how has it changed over time, and what are the long-term concerns related to the issue? How do interaction generalizations relate to your topic or issue? Develop a product of your choice (a model, a visual, media presentation) to teach the class about what you learn.

3. Revisit some of the questions you had the opportunity to debate. Create a presentation, brochure, advertisement, commercial, or poster for your community that expresses your position on the topic, using evidence from those who agree and disagree with your opinion. Use information from the unit concepts explored in class to support your ideas as well as your own research.

   ▪ Should trees be cut down to build homes or new communities?
   ▪ Should humans play a role in controlling the animal population?
   ▪ Should animals be kept in captivity?
   ▪ Should you kill spiders in your house?
   ▪ Should scientists step in to save endangered species?
   ▪ Should new species be introduced into the environment (e.g., frogs, ladybugs, elk and wolf populations in the American West, Asian carp in Lake Michigan, kudzu, reintroduced grizzly bears in Washington State, etc.)?

4. Consider the texts you have read, such as *The One and Only Ivan, Ivan: The Remarkable True Story of the Shopping Mall Gorilla*, poems, and picture books (*The Great Kapok Tree, The Other Side*). Choose at least three quotes or events from one of the texts, and explain how these relate to at least three scientific lesson ideas (e.g., food webs, ecosystems, overpopulation, energy transfer). Develop a visual (collage, poster, Prezi, Movie Maker, etc.) to illustrate and explain the connections you make between the science content of this unit

and the story quotes. Within your product, include the quote with an explanation of how it relates to a specific scientific idea from the unit. For example, Ivan says he has no one to protect. How does this relate to how animals interact in groups to survive?

5. Use the Science Wheel to explore a problem or potential problem and solution within an ecosystem in your area. Create a model that shows what might happen if the problem you are exploring becomes a reality. For example, you might explore ecosystems and interactions through issues that relate to the overpopulation of coyotes in your area, spraying to control for mosquitos to prevent the spread of disease to humans or animals, cutting down trees to build new communities, rerouting water sources, establishing community gardens in urban centers, building a subway or adding more busses on a bus route, etc. Then, brainstorm solutions that might work and test out the solutions using questions from the Science Wheel. Design a poster, movie, advertisement, infographic, or brochure that shows a model of the problem potential if not resolved, and then show your solution with a new model for how your solution will reduce the problem's impact. Be prepared to explain how you used the science wheel to analyze the problem and solution.

6. Design a piece of art about ecosystems that shows how interactions among various elements in art and the environment work to produce change. Write an artist summary for your piece that includes how colors, shapes, and perspective interact to create your image and how your image reflects a message about ecosystems.

7. Read through the following poem, "Ballad of the Tiger" by Ashley Hum, and independently complete a Blank Literary Analysis Wheel—Primary. Make connections between the poem and what you learned about ecosystems and interactions in *The One and Only Ivan*. Create a chart to show your comparisons.

Tiger, tiger, burning bright, fiery 'neath the starry night.
One day at noon, 12 o'clock, hunters came with box and lock.
Box and lock, lock and key, off to America, land of the free.
"Land of the free, but not for me. I am under lock and key."
Then to a zoo, in Waterloo, adults would come, and children too.
They'd come to look, and then to gawk, at a tiger, trapped by a lock.
This is how he came to be, a tiger from Africa, once wild and free.
From America, to Waterloo, the tiger was through.
Now he is trapped, under lock and key,
Yearning to be free.

—"The Ballad of the Tiger" by Ashley Hum

Note: Originally published in *Creative Kids* magazine, Winter 2012. Reprinted with permission of Prufrock Press.

ELA Task

Why are interactions important in ecosystems and literature? After reading the texts, analyzing art, and learning about science concepts in this unit, write at least three paragraphs to answer the question. Refer to at least three lesson ideas to develop your response and cite specific evidence from the materials explored throughout the unit.

Name: _____   Date: _____

Posttest
"The Wolf in Sheep's Clothing" *by Aesop*

Part I

Directions: Read the passage and respond to the following questions, citing evidence from the text. Complete the questions within 15 minutes, using a separate sheet of paper if necessary.

> A wolf had difficulty getting the sheep away from the shepherd and his dogs. But one day the wolf came upon the fleece of a sheep that had been sheared and thrown aside, so it put it on over its own pelt and strolled down among the sheep. Soon, the wolf in disguise was followed by a lamb. So, leading the lamb away from the shepherd and the flock, he soon made a meal of it—and for some time he succeeded in deceiving other sheep, enjoying hearty meals. Appearances can be deceiving.
>
> —"The Wolf in Sheep's Clothing" by Aesop

1. Explain how the different elements of the story (e.g., use of words, point of view, setting, characters, ideas, plot/conflict, images/symbols, etc.) help us understand the moral of the story.

2. Why did the wolf dress up like a sheep? Use evidence from the story to explain your answer.

3. How is what you know about interactions evident in the story? Use specific examples to support your ideas.

Part II

Directions: Develop a concept map about what you know about *ecology* on the back of this handout or on a separate sheet of paper.

4. Write *ecology* in the center, and draw spokes to other ideas related to ecology. You can add more connections to the new ideas you add.

   As you create a concept map, list all of the words you may know about the topic as separate boxes. The following words may be helpful. You do not need to use all of these words, and you may use other words you know as well: *environment, plants, animals, predators, prey, interactions, food chain, food web, pollination, habitat, change, energy, decomposer, omnivore, herbivore, carnivore, grow, live, die, adaptation*, etc.

   Make sure you show how the words you chose are related. Don't just write the words *habitat* and *change*, for example, as two different boxes on your map. Instead show connections by drawing lines between different words. Label the connections between the words you write. For example, you could draw a line to connect the words *habitat* and *change*, and then write a word that shows how they are related. Connect as many ideas together as you can.

Name: _____   Date: _____

Posttest Rubric
"The Wolf in Sheep's Clothing" *by Aesop*

	0	1	2	3	4
Question 1: Content: Literary Analysis	Provides no response.	Response is limited and vague. There is no connection to how literary elements contribute to the meaning or moral. A literary element is merely named.	Response is accurate with 1–2 literary techniques described with vague or no connection to a moral. Response includes limited or no evidence from text.	Response is appropriate and accurate, describing at least two literary elements and a moral. Response is literal and includes some evidence from the text.	Response is insightful and well-supported, describing at least two literary elements and how they enhance the moral. Response includes abstract connections and adequate evidence from the text.
Question 2: Process: Inference From Evidence	Provides no response.	Response is limited, vague, and/or inaccurate. The explanation or inference is not valid.	Response is accurate, but lacks adequate explanation. Response includes a weak inference.	Response is accurate and makes sense. Response includes a valid inference.	Response is accurate and well-written. Response includes a thoughtful and valid inference.
Question 3: Concept/Theme Applied to Literature	Provides no response.	Response is limited, vague, and/or inaccurate.	Response lacks adequate explanation. Response does not relate or create a generalization about interactions. Little or no evidence from text.	Response is accurate and makes sense. Response relates to or creates an idea about interactions with some relation to the text.	Response is accurate, insightful, and well-written. Response relates to or creates a generalization about interactions with evidence from the text.
Question 4: Content: Science	Provides no response.	Provides a limited number of examples of ecosystems or provides multiple examples that include inaccurate or irrelevant information.	Provides multiple and accurate examples but does not show relationships (or shows inaccurate relationships) among or between the examples listed.	Provides multiple examples and includes at least four accurate relationships among or between the examples provided.	Provides multiple examples and includes advanced and content-specific vocabulary with five or more accurate relationships among or between the examples provided.

Note: Adapted with permission from Stambaugh & VanTassel-Baska, 2011, and Center for Gifted Education, 2010.

Interactions in Ecology and Literature © Prufrock Press Inc.

References

Applegate, K. (2017). *The one and only Ivan* (Harper Classic ed.). New York, NY: HarperCollins.

Assouline, S., Colangelo, N., VanTassel-Baska, J., & Lupkowski-Shoplik, A. (Eds.). (2015). *A nation empowered: Evidence trumps the excuses holding back America's brightest students.* Iowa City: University of Iowa, The Connie Belin & Jacqueline N. Blank International Center for Gifted Education and Talent Development.

Biography.com Editors. (2017). *Georges Seurat.* Retrieved from https://www.biography.com/people/georges-seurat-9479599

Center for Gifted Education. (2010). *Dig it!: An earth and space science unit for high-ability learners (grade 3).* Waco, TX: Prufrock Press.

GeorgesSeurat.org. (2017). *Biography of Georges Seurat.* Retrieved from http://www.georgesseurat.org/biography.html

Kulik, J. A., & Kulik, C.-L. C. (1992). Meta-analytic findings on grouping programs. *Gifted Child Quarterly, 36,* 73–77.

M. C. Escher Foundation. (2017). *Biography.* Retrieved from http://www.mcescher.com/about/biography

National Governors Association Center for Best Practices, & Council of Chief State School Officers. (2010). *Common Core State Standards for English language arts.* Washington, DC: Author.

National Research Council. (2012). *A framework for K–12 science education: Practices, crosscutting concepts, and core ideas.* Washington, DC: The National Academies Press. https://doi.org/10.17226/13165

Rogers, K. B. (2007). Lessons learned about educating the gifted and talented: A synthesis of the research on educational practice. *Gifted Child Quarterly, 51,* 382–396.

Stambaugh, T., & VanTassel-Baska, J. (2011). *Jacob's Ladder Reading Comprehension Program: Level 4.* Waco, TX: Prufrock Press.

Steenbergen-Hu, S., Makel, M. C., & Olszewski-Kubilius, P. (2016). What one hundred years of research says about the effects of ability grouping and acceleration on K-12 students' academic achievement. *Review of Education Research, 86,* 849–899.

184

VanTassel-Baska, J. (1986). Effective curriculum and instruction models for talented students. *Gifted Child Quarterly, 30,* 164–169.

VanTassel-Baska, J., & Stambaugh, T. (2016). *Jacob's Ladder Reading Comprehension Program: Nonfiction, Grade 4.* Waco, TX: Prufrock Press.

Appendix A
Instructions for Using the Models

LITERARY ANALYSIS WHEEL—PRIMARY INSTRUCTIONS

The Literary Analysis Wheel—Primary is used to guide students through analyzing how an author uses literary techniques to develop meaning within a work. The model allows students to see connections between multiple literary elements (e.g., setting impacts conflict, conflict reveals character motives and values, characterization impacts theme, etc.).

Using the Literary Analysis Wheel—Primary

The Literary Analysis Wheel—Primary can be used to guide students through an analysis of a short story, poem, or novel. First, guide students to identify elements of the wheel separately, and then emphasize a deeper analysis by asking how elements relate to one other (e.g., point of view impacts theme, setting creates mood, etc.).

The Literary Analysis Wheel—Primary is meant to be interactive. The inner wheel conceptually spins so that its elements interact with each other and the outer wheel. Each element can relate to each other, regardless of its placement on the wheel.

The Literary Analysis Wheel—Primary Guide (Appendix B) shows specific prompts for each element of the wheel. The teacher may simply refer to the model during instruction or students may take notes on the Blank Literary Analysis Wheel—Primary using arrows to show how the various elements relate. It is suggested that students note the answers to the "simple" questions on the graphic organizer, and then discuss interactions with other elements. Consider making a poster of the Literary Analysis Wheel—Primary Guide and posting it in your classroom for students to refer to throughout the unit.

Once students are accustomed to using the wheel, encourage students to develop their own questions about the relationship between elements.

Students can make their own interactive paper-plate model of the wheel. Two different colored papers may be used for the inner and outer circles, secured with a brass paper fastener. Students may use the wheels as visuals in small groups.

Sample questions for literary analysis. The following questions can be asked to support students in analyzing literature. Note that complexity is added by combining elements.

- Simple:
  - **Characters:** *What are the values and motives of the characters? What evidence supports this? How does the author reveal character?*
  - **Setting:** *What is the time and place of the story?*
  - **Feelings of Author (Tone) and Reader (Mood):** *What are the author's feelings toward the subject (tone)? With what attitude does the author approach the theme (tone)? How do you feel as a reader and why (mood)?*
  - **Point of View:** *What is the narrator's point of view (first person, third person objective, third person limited, third person omniscient)?*
  - **Use of Words/Techniques:** *What figurative language and imagery does the author use? What is the author's style?*
  - **Conflict/Problem:** *What are the significant internal and external conflicts of the story? What is the main problem? What are the causes and effects of the problem?*
  - **Theme:** *What is the author's main message that can be generalized to broader contexts? (The theme is the author's point of view on a given subject.)*
  - **Sequence/Plot:** *What sequence of events occurs in the story? When and how is the conflict resolved?*

- Complex:
  - Setting+
    - *How does the setting influence the development of the theme?*
    - *How does the setting affect the reader's feelings?*
    - *What language does the author use to describe the setting (e.g., use of imagery, similes, etc.)?*
    - *How does the setting enhance conflict? How does the setting provoke plot events?*
    - *How is the setting symbolic of a larger idea (e.g., autumn, twilight)?*
    - *How does the setting affect and change the characters?*
    - *How does the setting help reveal the author's tone/attitude toward the theme/subject?*
    - *What conflicts could only happen in this setting? How does this influence the plot and theme?*

- Character+
  - *How do the characters' actions/beliefs/attitudes/struggles influence the theme?*
  - *How do the qualities of the characters affect the conflict as it relates to significant parts of the plot?*
  - *How do the characters' actions and responses establish emotion in the reader?*
  - *What characters' thoughts/feelings are hidden and/or revealed by the narrator's point of view? How does this impact the reader's experience of the story?*
  - *How does the author use language to develop character? Consider dialect, descriptions, use of figurative language, and names.*
  - *How does the setting affect character actions?*
  - *How does the author's tone toward the subject influence the development of characters?*

- Point of View+
  - *How does the narrator's point of view shape the theme?*
  - *How does the narrator's point of view establish emotions or feelings within the reader (e.g., the reader depends on the narrator's perspective in telling the story, so the reader feels the way the narrator does about what is being described)?*
  - *How does the narrator's point of view affect the way the reader views the significant conflicts and plot events?*
  - *What is the style of the narrator? How does the narrator's point of view (specifically, voice and diction) affect the story?*
  - *How is the author's tone revealed in the narrator's point of view (e.g., the narrator's words and feelings will reveal the attitude of how the author approaches the theme)?*
  - *How does the point of view of the story evoke feelings in you as a reader? Would the feelings you have be the same if told from a different point of view? Why or why not?*
  - *What character thoughts are revealed or hidden because of the narrator's point of view? How does this impact the reader's experience of the story?*

- Conflict/Problem+
  - *How does the conflict develop the theme? How would the theme be different if the conflict were resolved differently?*
  - *How does the conflict reveal the characters' values and motives?*
  - *How does setting impact the conflict and plot?*

- ◆ *What insight about the conflict does the reader have (or not have) as a result of the narrator's point of view?*
- ◆ *How do symbols represent aspects of the conflict (also consider foreshadowing devices)?*
- ◆ *How do character actions, thoughts, and conflicts reveal the author's tone?*
- ◆ *How does the plot and conflict reveal and/or change the mood?*
- ◆ *How does the author's style contribute to the development of the plot? Why does the author use more language/description on certain aspects of the plot than others?*

- Use of Words/Techniques+
  - ◆ *How does the author's use of figurative language or imagery contribute to literary elements?*
  - ◆ *How does the dialect of the characters contribute to our understanding of the characters?*
  - ◆ *How do various literary techniques inform our understanding of the author's style?*
  - ◆ *How does the use of words/techniques influence the mood?*

- Feelings of Author (Tone) and Reader (Mood)+
  - ◆ *How does the mood/tone help develop the theme? If the tone were different, how would this change the theme of the story?*
  - ◆ *How does the author's point of view help create mood?*
  - ◆ *How does the author's tone create mood for the reader?*
  - ◆ *How do the character's actions, thoughts, and conflicts contribute to the mood or tone?*
  - ◆ *How does the setting contribute to the mood?*
  - ◆ *How does the author use specific language to develop the mood or tone?*
  - ◆ *How do specific symbols help establish the mood or tone?*
  - ◆ *How is the author's tone revealed in the narrator's point of view (e.g., the narrator's words and feelings will reveal the attitude of how the author approaches the theme)?*
  - ◆ *What words/phrases does the author use to establish tone? How does the tone change throughout the story? How is this established through the author's style?*
  - ◆ *How is the author's tone revealed in the plot and conflicts? What specific textual evidence supports this?*
  - ◆ *How does the author's tone aid in developing the mood of the story?*
  - ◆ *How does the setting help reveal the author's tone/attitude toward the subject?*

- Sequence/Plot+
  - *How is the sequence/plot influenced by the conflict in the story?*
  - *How does the development of characters change as a result of the events in the sequence/plot?*
  - *How does the tone or mood change as a result of changes within the sequence/plot?*
  - *How does the author's use of words and techniques contribute to the development of the plot?*
  - *How does the setting of the story impact the sequence/plot? Would the sequence of the story change if the setting were different?*

- Structure and Style+
  - *How is the structure of the text influenced by the author's use of words/techniques?*
  - *How does the sentence structure impact the development of characters?*
  - *How is the conflict influenced by the use of dialogue?*
  - *How would the structure and style be impacted if the point of view changed?*
  - *How does the author's use of structure change throughout the sequence of the story?*
  - *How does the author's style help develop the problem and conflicts?*

- Theme+
  - *How does the plot impact the theme? How would the theme change if key parts of the plot or ending were changed?*
  - *How does the theme impact the development of the plot? If the author wanted to show a different theme, how would he or she have to change the plot of the story? How would the characters' values, motives, and actions change?*
  - *How does the author's choice of words contribute to the development of the theme?*

- Interpretation
  - *Taken altogether, what is your interpretation of the work (e.g., what is the explanation or meaning of this work given the author's use of various literary elements)? How did literary elements combine to create meaning? Support your interpretation by referring to the interaction of multiple elements in shaping your understanding of the work.*

Example Literary Analysis Lesson

Read the poem "Child Moon" by Carl Sandburg.

Step 1: Text-dependent questions. Lead students through a close reading of the text.

- What feelings can we associate with some of the words in this poem (wonder, crying, fading, babblings, golden)? Do the words promote feelings that are mostly positive or negative? (Sample response: The words create a mood that is mostly positive.)

- What is the author saying when he described the moon as "filtering on the leaves a golden sand"? (Sample response: The moonlight shines through the branches and looks like tiny flecks of light on the leaves, which might look like specks of sand.)

- After a second reading, students should respond to a partner: What is this poem about? (Sample response: The poem is about a little girl who is fascinated with the moon.)

- What makes this poetry? Does it rhyme? What makes this structure different from prose? What makes it different from other styles of poetry? (*Note*: Poetry expresses thoughts and ideas in a distinctive style, often through rhyme or rhythm.)

- How many sentences do you notice? What is important about the length of the sentences as they relate to the poem's ideas? (Sample response: The poem starts out with a short sentence, reflecting simplicity in the child's wonder. The next long sentence shows more of an elaborate description of the "thing," followed by an incomplete sentence showing how she falls back asleep, perhaps back from interrupted sleep to see the moon.)

- How does the lack of rhyme contribute to any literary elements (or meaning) of the poem? (Sample response: It evokes a sense of broken sleepiness, stream of conscious thought, as if following a child's thought process of the moon while half-awake.)

- Examine the first three lines of the poem. What contrast do you notice, and why is it significant? (Sample response: Young vs. old conveys the point of view of looking at something old through fresh eyes.)

- Why might the author refer to the moon as the "yellow thing"? Why is this important to the overall idea of the poem? (Sample response: This conveys more of the child's point of view, revealing more unknown wonder.)

- What are the major concepts or ideas in the poem? (Sample response: Wonder, innocence, perspective.) Literature, including poetry, reflects the human experience. What might the author want readers to consider about life? (Sample response: Appreciate the wonder of nature as a child appreciates it.)

Step 2. Literary Analysis Wheel—Primary, separate elements. Lead students through a simple analysis by completing the separate parts of the wheel.

- **Setting:** What is the setting? What words are used to describe the setting?
- **Characters:** Who is the main character in this poem? (Sample response: A young girl who is fascinated by the moon but not yet old enough to fully express herself.)
- **Point of View:** From what point of view is the poem written (first- or third-person point of view)? How would the poem be different if told from the first-person point of view of the little girl? (Sample response: It is in third-person point of view. We would know more of her specific thoughts about the moon if told from the girl's point of view.)
- **Use of Words/Techniques:** How does the author use words to develop imagery in the poem? (Sample response: Instead of saying moon, the author describes it as a "far silent yellow thing" and describes its light as "golden sand" on the leaves, which creates a visual image in your head of what the girl is seeing.)
- **Feelings of Author (Tone) and Reader (Mood):** What is the tone? (Sample response: His tone is positive. He is taken with her fascination of the moon.) What feelings does Sandburg produce for the reader? (Sample response: light-hearted, admiring mood.)
- **Sequence/Plot:** What is the sequence of events in the poem? (Sample response: A little girl sees the moon, cries out for it, and talks about it as she falls asleep.)
- **Structure and Style:** Is there a rhythm or rhyme to this poem? (Sample response: There is no rhyme or rhythm, an intentional decision on the part of the author.) Are the sentences complete? Why is this important? (Sample response: The incomplete sentence at the end conveys ideas of her thoughts as a child about to fall asleep.)
- **Theme:** What is the author's main message? (Sample response: Themes may relate to the power of wonder and fascination, nature's ability to fascinate in many different ways, view the wonder of nature through the eyes of a child, etc.)

Step 3. Combined elements for complexity. Discuss how multiple elements interact to establish an overall interpretation of the poem.

- **Use of Words/Techniques + Character:** How does Sandburg's use of language help develop our understanding of the character? (Sample response: The child points a finger and is "babbling" as she falls asleep. She also cries out with a little tongue. The child calls the moon a "yellow thing" and sees "golden sand" on the leaves. This would suggest that the character is very young and views the moon differently than adults.)

- **Setting + Use of Words/Techniques:** How is the setting developed by the use of words/techniques? (Sample response: The moon shines through the branches on the leaves, creating the appearance of golden sand.)
- **Sequence/Plot + Theme:** How does the sequence/plot impact the theme? (Sample response: The sequence of events, from the child pointing to the moon to babbling about it as she falls asleep, contributes to the idea that she is fascinated with nature. This helps establish the theme that she is fascinated by the wonder of nature, the moon).
- **Point of View + Mood:** How does the point of view affect the mood of the poem? (Sample response: The point of view is from a child, conveying an innocent, childlike, warm, lighthearted mood).
- **Structure/Style + Theme:** How does the author's structure (e.g., punctuation, rhyme scheme, etc.) contribute to the overall big idea of the poem? (Sample response: The lack of rhyme and fragmented sentences convey the thoughts of a child about to go to sleep; refer to the theme that the poem reminds the reader to appreciate nature through the eyes of a child.)

Literary Analysis Cubes

Younger students, or students who need more experience before working with the Literary Analysis Wheel—Primary, may choose to use literary cubes instead. Create cubes with a separate literary element written on each face of the cube, as indicated in Figure 3 (or see Appendix B). You may choose to tailor the words on each cube to focus on specific literary techniques with which students need more practice or focus.

Like the Literary Analysis Wheel—Primary, the cubes can be used to create simple and more complex questions and interactions. Students roll one cube and respond to how the text supports that element. Students may also roll two cubes and discuss how the two elements are related or interact. If the same word comes up on both cubes, students may ask their own question to the author about that feature and discuss it in their group. For example:

- Students roll "Point of View" on Cube 1 and "Theme" on Cube 2. Students may discuss how the author's point of view impacts the theme. They could ask, for example, how the theme of beauty is shown through the point of view of the narrator. The more specific the questions, the better.
- Students roll "Use of Words/Techniques" on Cube 1 and "Feelings of Author (Tone) and Reader (Mood)" on Cube 2. Students may discuss how the author uses different words or phrases or specific language features they know to create a feeling of sorrow.

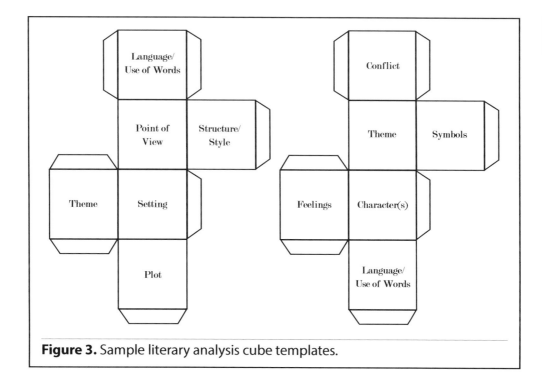

Figure 3. Sample literary analysis cube templates.

⬚   If duplicate words are rolled, such as Theme + Theme, students may discuss different themes present in the story, roll again, or manipulate the theme and discuss how another element would be affected.

See the Literature Analysis Wheel—Primary simple question examples as a guide. Although some of the words and key elements are different between the cubes and Literary Analysis Wheel, the use of simple and complex questions is the same. *Note*: Many teachers have found that it is helpful to print each cube in a different color to keep things organized.

VISUAL ANALYSIS WHEEL INSTRUCTIONS

The Visual Analysis Wheel is used to guide students through analyzing how an artist develops a main idea in art. Students analyze specific techniques, organization, and the artist's point of view toward the idea. Additionally, students examine prominent images and symbolism, the author's background, and emotions portrayed and evoked in the art. The model allows students to see the connection between multiple concepts (e.g., images are organized intentionally to create the main idea, point of view is influenced by the artist's background, specific techniques are used to evoke emotion, etc.).

Using the Visual Analysis Wheel

The Visual Analysis Wheel can be used to guide student through an in-depth analysis of art or visual media. It is meant to be interactive. The inner circle conceptually spins so that it interacts with elements on the outer circle.

The Visual Analysis Wheel Guide (Appendix B) shows specific prompts to guide students in thinking through each separate element. The teacher may simply refer to the model during instruction or students may take notes on the Blank Visual Analysis Wheel using arrows to show how the elements relate. It is suggested that students first note the answers to each concept separately on the graphic organizer, and then discuss how they influence each other.

Students can make their own interactive paper-plate model of the wheel. Two different colored papers may be used for the inner and outer circles, secured with a brass paper fastener. Students may use the wheels as visuals in small groups.

Sample questions for visual analysis. The following questions can be asked for analyzing art. Note that complexity is added by combining different elements.

- **Purpose/Context:**
  - *What is the purpose of the art?*
  - *What year was this art created? What artistic movements may have influenced this work? What type of art is this? What historical events were happening at the time this was made? Is there a specific audience for which the art was created?*

- **Main Idea:**
  - *What is the main idea of this art? What is the message of the art?*

- **Techniques:**
  - *What specific techniques does the artist use? (Consider color, shape, brushstroke, patterns, contrast.)*

- **Point of View:**
  - *What is the artist's point of view toward the topic?*
  - *What does the art reveal about the artist's beliefs?*
  - *What does the artist take for granted about the audience?*

- **Structure/Organization:**
  - *How does the artist organize ideas?*
  - *What is the central part of the painting?*
  - *Where is your eye drawn first? Why?*

▨ **Images:**
- *What are the main images?*
- *Why does the artist intentionally place the objects where they are?*
- *Do any of the images represent something other than the object itself? How?*

▨ **Images + Structure/Organization:**
- *Why does the artist intentionally place the objects where they are?*

▨ **Images + Point of View:**
- *What do the artist's images reveal about his or her point of view about the topic displayed?*

▨ **Images + Techniques:**
- *What specific techniques does the artist use to create the main images of the art?*

▨ **Images + Purpose/Context:**
- *How does the historical context influence the artist's choice of images in his art?*
- *How does the audience for which this is intended influence the artist's choice of images?*

▨ **Emotions:**
- *What emotions does this art make you feel?*
- *What emotions does this art reveal/portray?*

▨ **Emotions + Point of View:**
- *How does the artist's point of view toward the topic influence your emotional reaction to the art?*

▨ **Emotions + Techniques:**
- *What techniques does the artist use to portray and evoke emotion from his or her art?*

▨ **Emotions + Structure/Organization:**
- *Are parts of the art more emotionally powerful than others? How did the artist organize his or her painting to evoke or portray emotion?*

▨ **Emotions + Purpose/Context:**
- How does the historical situation influence how the artist expresses or evokes emotion?

- **Artist Background:**
  - *What do you know about the artist's personal life? Who influenced his or her work? How did his or her work influence others?*

- **Artist Background + Techniques:**
  - *What techniques does the artist use that are unique to his or her style?*

- **Artist Background + Point of View:**
  - *How does the artist's background influence his or her point of view/ assumptions about the topic?*

- **Artist Background + Structure/Organization:**
  - *Does the artist's background influence the way he or she organizes his or her art?*

- **Artist Background + Purpose/Context:**
  - *How is the artist influenced by the historical context of his or her time? How does the artist influence the historical context of his or her time?*

- **Implications:**
  - *What are the short- and long-term consequences of this art?*
  - *What are the implications for you after viewing this art?*

- **Evaluation:**
  - *Do you like this art? Why or why not? Use specific elements from the wheel in your answer.*
  - *What does this art make you think about? Would you hang this in your home? Why or why not?*
  - *What elements of this art are most important to consider and why?*

Example Visual Analysis Lesson

Students view the lithograph "Relativity" by M. C. Escher (available online). Do not reveal the title.

Step 1: Close viewing questions. Lead students through an initial viewing of the art.

- What detail of this art is interesting to you? (Ask every student; short response.)
- How many staircases are there? (Sample response: Seven; some overlap.)
- How many sources of gravity are in this picture? (Sample response: Three.)

- What behaviors do you see of the people?
- What is the focal point of the picture? Justify your answer.
- How does Escher produce "dual effects" on this painting? (Sample response: The ceiling is also a floor.) Note that though two people may be on the same staircase, they exist in two separate dimensions. Do they know of each other's existence? (Sample response: One is going up, one is going down, but they are going in the same direction.)
- Round-robin: If you had to give the lithograph a title, what title would you give it? (Ask every student; short response.)
- Share with your neighbor why you chose this title (or if time permits, elicit this as whole group).
- Share the real title of the lithograph, "Relativity." Why do you think Escher gave it this title?

Step 2. Visual Analysis Wheel, separate elements. Lead students through completing relevant parts of the Visual Analysis Wheel during discussion. Focus first on the separate elements.

- **Purpose/Context:**
  - *What is the context of this art?* Lithograph printed in 1953.
  - *What do you think his purpose/motive is in creating this?* To express an idea of reality. (*Note*: Students may not be able to determine this until after discussing the art to some extent.)

- **Point of View:**
  - *What is Escher's point of view toward reality?* Escher is revealing that there are multiple experiences and perceptions of reality. People perceive reality differently.

- **Images:**
  - *What do you believe are the most prominent images in the picture? Why? How might they be symbols for something deeper?* Staircases = journey in life; featureless people = unaware people, emotionless; windows to outside = ways to get out of isolation.
- **Emotions:**
  - *What emotions does this evoke in you? What emotions are revealed?* The featureless people reveal a lack of emotion, indicating that people are coming and going in life in an emotionless state.

- **Artist Background:**
  - *What do you know about the artist's background? How is the artist influenced by the historical context of his time?* M. C. Escher (1898–1972)

was a famous 20th-century Dutch artist who is known for developing impossible structures within his art. He made more than 448 lithographs (original prints) and woodcarvings, and more than 2,000 drawings (M. C. Escher Foundation, 2017). Escher also wrote many poems and essays, and he studied architecture, although he never graduated from high school. He used many mathematical aspects in his works. Most of Escher's works involve his own fascination with the concept of reality. His works showing paradoxes, tessellations, and impossible objects have had influence on graphic art, psychology, philosophy, and logic.

- **Main Idea:**
  - *What is Escher conveying about life in this painting? What is Escher's main idea?* Each person has his or her own view of reality and may be unaware of others' realities.

- **Implications:**
  - *What are the implications of this art on you the viewer?*

- **Evaluation:**
  - *Do you like this art? Would you hang it in your home? Does it make you think? Was the artist successful in presenting his ideas? Justify your answers with evidence.*

Step 3. Combined elements for complexity. Combine elements to develop more complex questions. Students may draw arrows on their wheels to show how elements relate (images + techniques, etc.).

- **Images + Techniques:**
  - *What techniques does Escher use to enhance images?* The people are all identical and featureless. There are three sources of gravity and seven stairways. The outside world is park-like. Some appear to be climbing upside down, but according to their gravity, they are climbing the staircase normally. Parts of the picture look two-dimensional; other parts look three-dimensional. He includes paradoxes (two people standing on the same staircase in separate realities). The basements add a surreal effect.

- **Images + Structure/Organization:**
  - *How does Escher intentionally place the objects in the painting to reveal meaning?* He purposefully draws two people standing on the same step (top center); they coexist yet they are in different gravity worlds. *What*

does this reveal about life? We are preoccupied with our own journeys; we do not acknowledge others' points of view.

- **Artist Background + Techniques:**
  - *What techniques does Escher use that are unique to his style?* Escher creates impossible realities within this work (three gravity worlds existing as one). He is known for creating paradoxes in his art.

- **Emotions + Structure/Organization:**
  - *How did the artist organize his art to portray or evoke emotion? What techniques were used to evoke or portray emotion?* It is interesting that the staircase structure is an upside-down triangle. Perhaps this is to give a more chaotic feel to the picture. Those within the staircases are "lost" in a world of coming and going, living life unaware beyond their own self-centered world. His technique of painting featureless people portrays a lack of emotion. The lack of emotion interplays with a main idea that the people are not aware of each other's existence, particularly in the other gravity worlds.

Visual Analysis Cubes

Younger students or students who need more experience before working with the Visual Analysis Wheel may choose to use visual analysis cubes instead. Create cubes with a separate visual element written on each face of the cube, as indicated in Figure 4 (or see Appendix B). You may tailor the words on each cube to focus on specific visual techniques for which students need more practice or focus.

Like the Visual Analysis Wheel, the cubes can be used to create simple and more complex questions and interactions. Students roll one cube and respond to how the visual supports that element. To add complexity, students may also roll two cubes and discuss how the two elements are related or interact. If the same word comes up on both cubes, students may ask their own question to the illustrator about that feature and discuss it in their group. For example:

- Students roll "Visual Effects" on Cube 1 and "Feelings" on Cube 2. Students may discuss: How does the artist's choice of color (visual effect) evoke emotion in you?
- Students roll "Structure" on Cube 1 and "Image" on Cube 2. Students may discuss: Why are the images placed where they are (structure)?
- If duplicate words are rolled, such as Structure + Structure, students may compare the structure of another piece of art they know to the art piece or roll again.

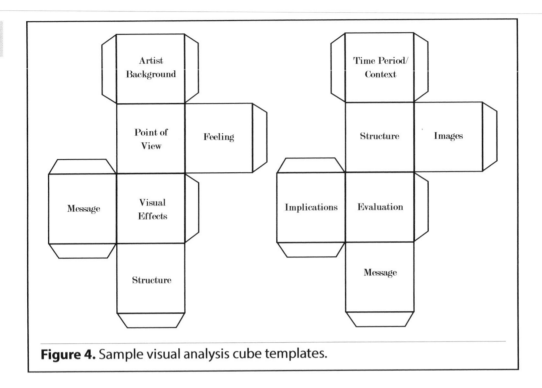

Figure 4. Sample visual analysis cube templates.

See the Visual Analysis Wheel simple and complex question examples as a guide. Although some of the words and key elements are different between the cubes and the Visual Analysis Wheel the use of simple and complex questions is the same. *Note*: Many teachers have found that it is helpful to print each cube in a different color to keep things organized.

TEXT ANALYSIS WHEEL—PRIMARY INSTRUCTIONS

The Text Analysis Wheel—Primary is used to help students analyze the development of a main idea. Similar to the Literary and Visual Analysis Wheels, students read an informational text and complete the individual components of the wheel, including the author's points with evidence, main idea or message, point of view, assumptions, techniques/structure, context/audience/vocabulary, and implications, and evaluation. Then students examine how the features of the text interact. These questions are adapted from and support the CCSS for ELA Informational Text Standards (National Governors Association for Best Practices & Council of Chief State School Officers, 2010).

- **Main Idea or Message:** What is the main idea or message of this text?

- **Point of View:**
  - What is the author's point of view toward the topic?
  - What other points of view or texts need to be considered?
  - What facts are included? Are these accurate? What opinions are included?
  - How does my point of view differ or agree with the text?
  - Is this fact or opinion? What biases might be present?

- **Techniques/Structure:**
  - How is the information structured?
  - What techniques are used?
  - How does the author use emotions or story to help convey meaning?
  - How does the author use arguments or facts to help convey meaning?
  - How does the author use or refer to experience or expertise to help convey meaning?
  - What can you learn from the headings, illustrations, charts, or graphs? How are these used?
  - How does the author explain cause-effect relationships? How does the author show comparisons, sequencing, chronological order, problem-solution ideas, or basic information?
  - How does the author show the relationship between people, events, and ideas?

- **Context/Audience/Purpose:**
  - When was this written? Is this current? How do you know?
  - How should you interpret this?
  - What is the purpose of this text?
  - Who was this written for?
  - What words do you need to know, define, or draw in order to understand the text?

- **Supporting Details:** What details are used to support the author's message or main idea? Why are these details important to include?
- **Implications:** What are the implications of ___? What are the short-term and long-term implications? Positive and negative implications?

Complex Questions:
- **Point of View+**
  - **Supporting Details:** What details reveal bias? Do some of these details make you change your point of view?

- **Techniques/Structure:** How does the author's use of emotion help you understand the author's point of view? Do you agree or disagree with the author's presentation of facts/arguments?
- **Context/Audience/Vocabulary:** Because the purpose of the text is to ___ (explain, persuade, inform, entertain), how does this influence the author's presentation of facts and opinions? What other points of view should be considered that might relate to the given audience?
- **Main Idea/Message:** Do you agree with the main idea or message in the text? Why or why not?

- **Techniques/Structure+**
  - **Supporting Details:** Why are the details organized in this way? Which details relate to emotion or story? Which details relate to developing arguments and presenting facts? Which details relate to the use of experience or expertise? How do the text features help us understand the organization of the supporting details?
  - **Point of View:** Are the text-features (e.g., graphs) accurate or do they convey bias? When the author discusses the relationship between a person, idea, or event, how does this help us understand the author's point of view?
  - **Context/Audience/Purpose:** How does the author use text-features to help readers understand vocabulary? Why is the text organized in this way for this particular audience?
  - **Main Idea/Message:** How does the structure of the text help the audience understand the main idea?

- **Context/Audience/Purpose+**
  - **Supporting Details:** What details convey the author's purpose? What details help us understand the context (what is happening)?
  - **Point of View:** What does the author consider about the audience's point of view? How do you know?
  - **Techniques/Structure:** How does the author's use of emotion, argument, or expertise/experience help the audience understand the main idea? How do these elements support the author's purpose?

Example Text Analysis—Primary

After reading the text, "Jane Goodall" (see p. 205), lead students through completing relevant parts of the Text Analysis Wheel—Primary. Students do not need to write detailed explanations on the organizer, just notes. Focus first on separate elements, then combine elements to develop more complex questions. Students may draw arrows on their wheels to show how elements relate (Point of View + Techniques/Structure, etc.).

- **Main Idea or Message:** What is the main idea or message of this text? (Sample response: Jane Goodall made significant contributions to our understanding of chimpanzees.)
- **Point of View:** What facts are included? Are these accurate? (Sample response: Several facts are listed about her life experiences and her interactions with chimpanzees. To check for accuracy, the text could be compared to other sources.) What other points of view should be considered? (Sample response: Because the article mentions her concerns about the unethical treatment of chimpanzees in research and the destruction of their habitats, it would be important to understand why researchers use these practices and why mining and logging might be important to other groups.)
- **Context/Audience/Purpose:** What is the purpose of the article? For whom do you think this was written? (Sample response: To inform readers about the contributions of Jane Goodall. This was probably written to help readers understand the importance of her work and possibly influence their points of view about the importance of the natural world.) How should you interpret the text? (Goodall had a strong childhood interest that developed into a passion, which led to major contributions for understanding animal behaviors; students may explore this idea as it relates to their personal interests.) What words do you need to know to understand this text? What places should we locate on a map to help us understand more about Goodall's life?
- **Techniques/Structure:** How is the information structured? (The text is organized in chronological order, starting with her experiences, from childhood through her lifetime.) In what ways does the author include cause-effect within the text? (Sample response: The author describes a series of cause-effect relationships. Goodall's early interests caused her to study animals, particularly chimps. Her interactions with chimps had a major effect on our understanding of animal behavior, etc.) How does the author use emotion or story? (Sample response: The author describes the banana club experience, which helps the reader understand the close and personal interactions with the chimps.) What does the image convey about Jane Goodall? (Sample response: She appears to have wisdom and insight about her passion. The folded hands convey a sense of reverence for her work.)
- **Supporting Details:** What are the three most important supporting details of the text that help enhance the main idea? (Sample response: Details about her early education experiences, details about her research and insight about chimpanzee behaviors, details about her contributions beyond her immediate interactions with the chimps.)

Complex Questions:

- **Techniques/Structure + Supporting Details:** Why are the details placed in chronological order? How does this help us understand the main idea better? How would our understanding of her contributions be different if the article only included her contributions from the 1970s–1980s? (Sample response: We would not have an understanding of her close interactions with the chimpanzees, nor would we have insight about her passions and interest in animals she had as a child.)

- **Context/Audience/Purpose + Point of View:** What words convey Goodall as a positive influence on the world? Does the author present any of Goodall's flaws? How would the inclusion of her strengths and weaknesses change our interpretation of the main idea? (Sample response: If the author had included strengths and weaknesses, it could have allowed the reader to see more of the struggles she faced as she made her contributions.)

- **Supporting Details + Supporting Details:** How do the details about her childhood help enhance our understanding of the details about her older years? (Sample response: This conveys the idea that her fascination with animals lasted a lifetime; she was able to make meaningful contributions to the world.)

- **Text/Structure + Point of View:** Why are the facts about her interactions and games with the chimps so important? How does that influence the reader's point of view towards her? (Sample response: The humorous experience of her playing banana games with the chimpanzees might build a connection with the reader.)

- **Point of View + Main Idea:** To what extent has your point of view about animal habitat preservation changed as a result of reading this text?

- **Implications + Main Idea:** What are the long-term implications of Jane Goodall's experiences with chimps? How could you put into action some of the ideas presented in the text? What do you think the organization "Roots and Shoots" might do to extend her legacy (students may research for further exploration)?

JANE GOODALL[1]

Jane Goodall is a prominent primatologist and animal rights activist. During her many years observing chimpanzees in Tanzania, she revolutionized popular understanding of humans' relationship to chimps.

Jane was always a natural animal lover. Born in London, England in 1934, she grew up fascinated with animals. Once, when she was just 4 years old, her parents reported her missing. Later, they found her sitting in the henhouse studying the hens and trying to learn how they laid their eggs. She observed all kinds of animals in her neighborhood, taking notes and drawing sketches. She dreamed of traveling to Africa to meet the animals she read about in her books.

Jane attended a private school, where she received her certificate in 1950. At age 18, she left school and became a secretary at Oxford University. During this time, she also worked in the film industry, hoping to save up money to live in Africa. Finally, at the invitation of a friend, Jane took her first trip to Africa. There she came into contact with anthropologist Louis Leakey, the curator of the Coryndon Museum in Nairobi, who soon hired her as a secretary.

Leakey had always wanted to study primate behavior over a long-term period. He hoped that this kind of study could help scientists better understand evolution, particularly the development of the chimpanzee. Previous studies of chimps had failed; researchers either scared chimps away when they approached or simply did not spend enough time with them. Leakey saw a solution in Jane's gentle and patient personality, and asked her to work with chimps on the Gombe Stream Reserve. Some experts criticized his decision; Jane had no college degree or formal training with primates. But her passion for observation and attention to detail would prove them wrong.

Jane's first trips to observe the chimps failed—they would run away when she came too close to their feeding grounds—so she established a daily pattern of watching from a distance in the mornings. Bit by bit, she worked her way closer to their habitat, and within a year, she could watch the chimps from within 30 ft. After 2 years, they allowed her even closer. By that point, chimps would approach her looking for bananas!

After gaining the trust of the chimps, Jane established the "banana club," a daily feeding ritual in which she would imitate chimp movements, spend time in trees,

[1]*Note*: This article is from *Jacob's Ladder Reading Comprehension Program: Nonfiction, Grade 4* (pp. 29–30), by J. VanTassel-Baska and T. Stambaugh, 2016, Waco, TX: Prufrock Press. Copyright 2016 by Prufrock Press. Reprinted with permission.

and eat their foods. Through this method, she became close with many of members of the group and made astonishing discoveries.

Jane was the first researcher to observe chimpanzees using tools. Until that time, humans had believed that the ability to create and use tools separated us from the rest of the animal kingdom. But the chimps showed the ability to manipulate objects to suit their needs. For example, they would modify leaves and use them to lure termites from their hills. They would then use the leaves like spoons to eat the termites. Jane also discovered that the chimps ate meat. They had previously been classified as vegetarian, but Jane saw the chimps kill and eat insects, birds, and some small mammals.

Most importantly, Jane observed that chimps had a complex social system with rituals and communication methods. They had familial bonds and would embrace each other during times of mourning. They also communicated to each other using a primitive system of sounds. Chimpanzees were far more complex than we had thought.

During the 1960s, Jane spent only a little time away from the reserve. She took trips to the University of Cambridge to complete her Ph.D. in ethology, the science of animal behavior. She was one of very few students in the history of Cambridge to pursue an advanced degree without first earning an undergraduate degree.

In the 1970s, Jane became concerned about the habitat and well-being of the chimps she was studying. Increased mining and logging were threatening the habitats of many African animals. She became involved in educating the public, working with businesses and local governments to encourage ecological responsibility. She also spread the word about the unethical treatment of chimpanzees in research studies.

Jane has won countless awards and toured all over the world. The Jane Goodall Institute, established in 1977, promotes ecotourism, health, and sustainable agriculture. Even kids can get involved through Roots and Shoots, a youth-led community action program. Now in her 80s, Jane continues to help us understand and engage with the natural world around us.

REFERENCES

Bagley, M. (2014). Jane Goodall biography. *LiveScience*. Retrieved from http://www.livescience.com/44469-jane-goodall.html

Biography.com. (n.d.). *Jane Goodall*. Retrieved from http://www.biography.com/people/jane-goodall-9542363

SCIENCE ANALYSIS WHEEL INSTRUCTIONS

The Science Analysis Wheel is used to guide students through analyzing how scientists use various elements to approach and solve problems and issues that are grounded in specific content. The wheel allows students to see connections between concepts (e.g., patterns, cause and effect, systems, interactions and relationships, evidence, findings, etc.) that cut across scientific content (National Research Council, 2012). For a more detailed explanation of the crosscutting concepts used in the Next Generation Science Standards, visit http://ngss.nsta.org/ CrosscuttingConceptsFull.aspx.

Using the Science Analysis Wheel

The Science Analysis Wheel can be used to guide students through an analysis of issues relevant to the content they are studying. First, guide students to identify elements of the wheel separately, and then emphasize a deeper analysis by asking how elements relate to one another (e.g., Cause and Effect impacts Findings, Scale and Proportion influences Process, etc.).

The Science Analysis Wheel is meant to be interactive. The inner wheel conceptually spins so that its elements interact with each other and the outer wheel. Each element can relate to each of the others, regardless of its placement on the wheel. The Science Analysis Wheel Guide shows specific prompts for each element of the wheel. The teacher may simply refer to the model during instruction, or students may take notes on the Blank Science Analysis Wheel using arrows to show how the various elements relate. It is suggested that students note the answers to the "simple" questions on the graphic organizer, and then discuss interactions with other elements. Consider making a poster of the Science Analysis Wheel Guide and posting it in your classroom for students to refer to throughout the unit.

Once students are accustomed to using the wheel, encourage students to develop their own questions about the relationships between elements. Students can also make their own interactive paper-plate model of the wheel. Two different colored papers may be used for the inner and outer circles, secured with a brass paper fastener. Students may use the wheels as visuals in small groups.

The innermost circle of the Science Analysis Wheel is multifaceted, as the wheel may be used to analyze a hypothesis, an idea, a problem, or a question. For example, the wheel could be used to ask a simple question about how phases of the moon affect tides or to test a hypothesis or solution to a problem, such as what might happen if a new species was introduced into the environment or if people stopped watering plants.

The top of the wheel labeled "Real-World Issue or Problem" allows students to think about a broad question that relates to a more specific question/

hypothesis/problem in the center wheel. For example, if students are using the wheel to study the question "How are clouds formed?" (the center wheel), a real-world issue might be "How do clouds affect the weather?" or perhaps "How does air pollution affect the formation of clouds?" In another example, students might hypothesize that a given ratio of glue to borax is the best ratio for making a polymer substance (the center wheel). The real-world issue might be: How can polymers be engineered to make materials stronger and more durable? The Science Analysis Wheel can also be applied to engineering. Students may be asked to design or invent a prototype that uses nanotechnology. In the inner wheel, students might write their idea (e.g., nanotechnology applied to clothing that monitors a specific health condition). The real-world issue might be, "How can nanotechnology improve our lives?" The real-world issue is directly related to students' hypothesis, solution idea, issue, or question.

Sample questions for science analysis. The following questions can be asked to support students as they analyze problems grounded in science content. Note that complexity is added by combining elements.

Simple Questions:

- **Idea/Hypothesis Question:** What solution idea should be tested? What is your hypothesis? What question do you have about the problem, issue, or topic? What do you need to know? What do you want to know?
- **Cause and Effect:** What cause-and-effect relationships exist within the problem or hypothesis? What evidence supports the causality? What are multiple causes of the phenomenon? What are the multiple effects of the problem? Of the solution? What contributes to the cause-effect relationships? How does cause-effect allow for prediction? Engineering: How can you design cause-effect?
- **Systems/Energy and Matter:** How does energy or matter flow in and out of the system you are exploring? How does the flow of energy or matter help you understand the issue or topic you are exploring? How is energy transferred within the system you are exploring? What are the inputs, outputs, interactions, and boundaries of the system? What elements of a system need to be considered when___? What subsystems influence the larger system? How? How do external systems affect this system?
- **Stability and Change:** What changes have occurred as a result of ___? What causes or prohibits stability in ___? What natural systems create stability or change? How does ___ affect stability/change in ___? What does not change?
- **Patterns:** What patterns do you notice? How can you model or graph this to show trends? How would you classify or categorize this information? What can you predict from these patterns? How does this pattern help us understand relationships between__ and__?

- **Scale and Proportion:** How can you measure or quantify ____? What scale is being used to inform your understanding of the issue? To what extent does the scale influence ____? What is the magnitude of ____? What is the best way to measure____? What is the effect of length of time on ____?

- **Structure and Function:** What are the parts? What are the functions? How does the structure of ____ determine ____? How is a ____ (living or non-living thing) shaped based on its structure? What substructures determine ____ (properties or functions)? How are the parts related?

- **Scientific Information:** What are the existing scientific principles that relate to the issue? What are the guiding assumptions? What rules, laws, and theories need to be considered? What additional topics in science are connected to the issue or hypothesis being explored? What relevant concepts/topics do you need to study or apply to ____? What other scientific explanations need to be considered?

- **Evidence/Data:** What questions do you have about ____? What data are informing your questions? How do your evidence/data support or refute the findings of others? What data or evidence do you need to collect in order to ____? What inferences can you make? What can you predict from this data?

- **Perspectives/Audience:** What other perspectives need to be considered as you begin to explore your problem/hypothesis? What perspective are you considering now? How might different scientists look at this differently? Who is the intended audience? What process would a ____ (type of scientist) follow to ____? What process do you need to follow? Have you considered or examined perspectives that do not agree with your ideas? What are the pros and cons of various perspectives?

- **Findings/Solutions:** What do you do next with your findings? What inferences can you make about ____? How do you communicate or model your findings or ideas? How would the outcome be different if a different variable or element were isolated or studied? What other solutions have worked? What are the limitations of your findings? Of others' findings? To what extent can these findings be generalized or applied to broader contexts or other populations?

- **Modeling:** How can you model your thinking in a way that shows what will or might happen as a result of____? How can you best create a model to represent your ideas (diagram, prototype, analogy, illustration)? How might you evaluate, test, or revise your model? What are the limitations of your model?

- **Process/Methods:** What processes or methods are most suitable for solving the problem or testing your hypothesis? Which variables or changes are you isolating for study? Are your methods articulated in a way that allows for replication? Are your methods fair? What are the limitations and flaws to your methods?

Complex Questions:

■ **Cause and Effect+:**
- What short- and long-term implications does the cause-effect relationship have on _____?
- How do cause-effect relationships have an effect on the flow of energy or matter within a system?
- How do negative or positive cause-effects impact stability or change within a system?
- In what ways can your understanding of the impact of certain effects be influenced by a change in scale or perspective?
- How might you measure or quantify the cause-effect relationship?
- What cause-effect relationships are necessary to achieve balance, stability, or change within a system?
- What causes the flow of energy or matter within a system to change, and what impact does that have on the existing system?
- How is the flow of energy and matter within a system influenced by changes in cause-effect relationships?
- What patterns can be found within the cause-effect relationship?
- How do patterns help you understand underlying cause-effect relationships?
- How do scientific theories and relevant concepts influence your understanding of the cause-effect relationships?
- How is data influenced by changes in the cause-effect relationship?
- How might the cause-effect relationship be explained differently if examined from an alternative perspective?
- How can you create a model to represent the cause-effect relationship?
- What inferences can be made about the cause-effect relationship?

■ **Systems/Energy and Matter+:**
- How do interactions within a system lead to stability within the system? How does the flow of energy or matter lead to stability or change within a system?
- What patterns can be found within the system, and how do they influence the flow of energy and matter?
- What cause-effect relationships exist within the system? How do those relationships influence the flow of matter or energy?
- How do interactions among living and nonliving objects influence the flow of energy and matter within the system?

- How do changes to the existing structure and functions impact the overall system?
- What scientific theories and relevant concepts influence your understanding of the system?
- What evidence can be gathered about the system's inputs and outputs? How does energy and matter flow in and out of the system?
- How do scientists from different fields look at this system differently?
- What does the system have in place to develop structure and function? What impact do those structures have on the balance within the system?
- What systems are in place to allow for interactions that promote stability or change? How is stability or change managed within the system?
- How are systems dependent on interactions and relationships? How is a system disrupted by changes in interactions and relationships?
- How does perspective influence understanding of a system? What processes exist within a system and how are these influenced by interactions and relationships?
- What inferences can be made about the way that energy and matter flow within the system? How would the system change if one of the inputs or outputs were changed?
- How does the study of the function and malfunction within the system help inform solution ideas?
- How might you design a model to communicate with others how the parts of a system interact?

- **Stability and Change+:**
  - If we remove one element from the system, how does the system adapt or change?
  - How do stability and change influence systems?
  - What interactions and relationships need to exist in order for stability to occur? How does a system maintain equilibrium?
  - How does stability within a system change when scale/proportion are increased or decreased? Does a change in scale lead to a change in stability? What short- and long-term consequences does change in scale have on the stability of a system?
  - What causes stability or change within a system? What effect does stability or change have on the system?
  - How does stability or change impact the flow of energy or matter?
  - How does stability depend on interactions and relationships? How does a disruption in those relationships and interactions lead to change?
  - What relationship exists between stability and change and structure and function? What happens when the relationship changes?

- How do structure and function promote stability? How do they promote change?
- What patterns exist within the system to lead to stability? Why are patterns necessary for stability?
- What scientific theories or concepts contribute to the understanding related to stability and change within a system?
- What evidence is needed in order to understand the systems needed to ensure stability?
- As you investigate your hypothesis or question, what variables must not change in order to test effects?
- How might you construct a model to show how ____ maintains stability? How might you construct a model to show how ____ enables change?

Patterns+:
- What patterns emerge in your data, and how do they influence findings?
- What patterns exist when scale is changed? What relationship exists between patterns and proportion?
- How do patterns help establish or promote stability or change within a system?
- What patterns exist to influence structure and function?
- How are patterns used to support or inform scientific theories?
- How does the development of patterns influence findings, solutions, and models?
- How can patterns influence perspective and process?
- How do patterns help us make predictions about the outputs of a system? About change and stability within a system? About cause-effect within a system?
- How is the interaction of patterns and evidence used in the development of future questions?
- How can you design a model to accurately predict and describe patterns?

Scale and Proportion+:
- What are the implications of changing the scale that is used?
- How does the scale that is used influence findings?
- How does the proportion of elements within a system influence stability or change?
- How would cause-effect relationships change within a system if scale were altered?
- How does scale and proportion influence the flow of matter and energy within a system?

- How can you design a model to convey the scale and proportion of ___? What measurement system should be used in your modeling?

Structure and Function+:
- What impact does structure or function have within a system?
- How do scientific concepts and theories inform our understanding of structures, substructures, and related functions?
- How does structure impact existing patterns within a system?
- What happens to structure and function as scale or proportion is changed?
- How is the flow of energy and matter managed within the structure?
- How do the structure and function promote stability and change? Why does stability matter within structure, and what consequences exist when function or structure changes?
- How are subsystems and systems impacted by changes within existing structures?
- How can structures create cause-effect relationships?
- What relationship exists between structure and systems?
- How does structure promote the development of patterns within a system?
- What is the relationship between the structure and scientific theories and relevant concepts needed to understand the issue or hypothesis?
- What evidence is needed to understand structure and the changes within a system? What questions need to be asked in order to understand structure and function?
- How can structures be understood from multiple perspectives? What impact does process have on understanding the interaction between structure and function?
- How do structural components influence the way findings are used to develop solutions or inform questions?
- How might you create a model to represent the structure, parts, function, and interaction of parts?

Scientific Information+:
- How do the scientific theories and concepts help inform your hypothesis?
- How does change in scale/proportion support or refute scientific theories and relevant concepts?
- What can you predict the outcome of this problem will be, based on the scientific information you know or have read?
- How do cause-effect relationships influence scientific theories, and what impact do changes in these relationships have on _____?

- How do scientific theories and concepts support the need for stability or change within the system?
- How does the function of _____ relate to the theory of _____?
- How does this scientific information impact my methods for testing a new idea?
- How do existing theories about the topic or system differ based on perspectives?
- Has your idea been tested before, and if so, what were the outcomes or information available about this? Would these outcomes be the same under different conditions?
- How do your new findings connect with or influence the current scientific theories?
- How might you design a model to represent the scientific concepts that influence prediction, explanation, or revision of the theories?

Evidence/Data+:

- What evidence do you need to collect in order to answer your question or support your hypothesis?
- How is evidence informed by patterns that exist within a system?
- How are data influenced by changes in the cause-effect relationship?
- How do these data help predict cause-effect relationships?
- What methods should you use to test and analyze your data?
- What evidence can be gathered about the system's inputs and outputs? What evidence can be gathered about the flow of energy and matter in and out of the system?
- How does the evidence point to the need for stability and change within a system?
- How might you measure and quantify your data? What are the limitations to the processes used to collect data?
- What evidence is needed in order to determine whether or not your idea will allow for stability or positive change?
- What evidence is needed to understand structure and the changes within a system? What questions need to be asked in order to understand structure and functions?
- How does evidence support or refute existing scientific theories and relevant concepts? What impact do new data have on the questions asked with regard to scientific theories?
- How do different audiences interpret and ask different questions? How does their interpretation influence the findings or solutions?
- How will you communicate how your data answers your questions or informs your hypothesis through an accurate model?

Perspectives/Audience+:
- How might various perspectives view the problem differently? What other questions might other types of scientists ask? How would this solution idea affect various groups of people?
- How does perspective shape the questions asked and evidence gathered?
- In what way does the process used to collect data or explore an issue influence findings? How does perspective influence the way in which models are used?
- How does perspective influence the scale that is used? Does process determine proportion, or does proportion determine process in experimental design?
- How does the perspective of the individual shape the way in which scientific information is applied to the hypothesis/problem?
- What process is used to test the hypothesis or explore the issue? What are the limitations to the methods as applied to the hypothesis? How does the selected process influence the patterns that are discovered?
- How might perspective influence one's understanding of a system and the significance of various inputs, outputs, and boundaries? Why is it beneficial to explore a system from multiple perspectives?
- How does perspective influence the ways in which interactions are observed, either as positive, negative, or mutually beneficial?
- What might be revealed about a scientist's perspective through the cause-effect relationships documented in findings?
- How can exploring an issue through different perspectives or processes lead to confirmation or changes in the way hypotheses and issues are understood?
- How would the types of models used look different for various audiences? For what audiences is it best to present an illustration? An analogy? A prototype? A diagram?

Findings/Solutions+:
- What other solutions have been used to solve similar problems that you might adapt? How can the limitations and flaws within others' findings help improve the processes you use to investigate your question?
- How does the evidence that is gathered influence findings?
- How can various solutions bring about stability or change within the problem being explored?
- What models exist to support/reflect existing scientific theories?
- How can perspective influence the way that findings are used to develop solutions or create models?

- How can observed patterns be used to understand findings and influence solutions?
- How can a change in scale impact the solution? How can a solution change based on scale?
- How can you use or apply a model to develop a solution? How might you revise a current model so that it works as a solution to my problem?
- How might you communicate your findings or solution through an accurate model?

▪ **Process/Methods+:**
- What processes need to be considered when examining the influence of causal relationships within a system?
- How does changing one variable within the experiment or process for data collection impact the findings and solutions?
- How do the process and method used within an experiment influence the evidence that is collected and the questions that are asked?
- How does the process used to collect data influence the findings?
- How does perspective influence the method for data collection?
- How can a model help inform the methods and processes of studying a scientific phenomenon?
- How can I communicate my methods within a model so they are replicable?

▪ **Modeling+:**
- How can you develop a model to show the interactions within a system or the flow of energy and matter within a system?
- How can you develop a model that might be used to predict cause-effect and change within a system?
- How might you apply scientific theories to your model? How do scientific theories inform your approach to your model?
- What evidence or data are needed to test the efficacy of your model?
- How might you develop a model to show visual, mathematical, or graphic representations of trends you observe in your data?
- How would different perspectives view the limitations of your model?
- How does scale and proportion affect the usefulness and accuracy of the model?

Example Science Analysis Wheel Lesson

Within this example, students are exploring the impact that imbalances or over-/underpopulation of a species have on an ecosystem. Students are presented with a scenario related to wild boar population growth. They are asked to complete a table and graphing exercise to examine and model how the population of wild boars and the availability of the food they eat has changed over time. They will notice an inverse relationship in the boar growth and plant scarcity. (See Lesson 7 for full details relating to the scenario, graphing exercise, and debriefing.)

Step 1: Activity-dependent questions.

- What does this graph assume about the boars included in the population? What does it assume about the growth and life cycle of the tubers? (Sample response: The boar population is only affected by the hunters, birth of new boars, and loss due to starvation.)
- What additional information would we need in order to understand the devastation that might occur within the ecosystem? (Sample response: You would need to know how other living and nonliving organisms are affected.)
- What are the short- and long-term consequences that the boar population increase would have on the food web and ecosystem the boars are a part of? (Sample response: Overpopulation of the boars would disrupt the food web because the boars would eat too many of the producers lower down on the food chain, making it harder for other consumers to find food.)
- What evidence suggests that humans should intervene and play a greater role in controlling animal populations? What additional information would you need to support your decision? What perspectives are missing? (Sample response: The boar population is disrupting their own ecosystem and impacting food webs and chains. Farmland and crops are also being impacted. The perspectives of ecologist, hunter, farmer, etc., would need to be considered.)
- What new questions do you have that would help you make a responsible decision regarding the boar population? (Sample response: How many other organisms are being impacted by the boars? How have other species' overpopulation situations been handled?)
- What are the reasons that some people might not want humans to intervene in animal populations? (Sample response: There may be positive consequences to the boar population for the ecosystem.)
- If a decision were made to increase the number of hunted boars per year, should hunters target male or female boars? Why does a decision like this matter? What consequences could this have on the ecosystem? (Sample response: They should target the female boars because they are having multiple litters of new boars each year. However, if you target only females, the imbalance between male and females may have negative consequences.)
- What does the graph tell you about the severity of the problem (i.e., the potential for catastrophic ecosystem damage)? (Sample response: The pop-

ulation growth escalated quickly, and as a result almost wiped out the tubers available in the ecosystem.)

- Based on the information you gathered, what would you tell the department of wildlife about the severity of the wild boar problem on the ecosystem? Why? (Sample response: I would tell the department of wildlife to issue more hunting licenses and encourage hunters and farmers to trap and kill female boars. If the female boar population is controlled there will be fewer new boars added each year.)

Step 2: Science Analysis Wheel, separate elements. Lead students through a simple analysis by completing the separate parts of the wheel.

- **Real-World Issue/Problem:** Should humans intervene to control the increase or decline of animal populations?
- **Idea/Hypothesis/Question:** How does the wild boar population impact the ecosystem?
- **Scientific Information:** What do you know about ecosystems that might help you answer this question? (Sample response: Ecosystems require a balance between organism populations. Overpopulation of consumers can have a detrimental effect on the producers within an ecosystem.)
- **Evidence/Data:** What can you predict might happen to the ecosystem if humans allowed the wild boar population to get out of control or decline? What do the data you collected with the graphing activity suggest? What new data might you collect to help you understand how big this problem is? (Sample response: I might collect new data on the populations of other producers and consumers within the ecosystem to see what sort of effect the boar population growth is having. If humans allow the boar population to grow, a prediction could be made that the tuber population would be wiped out, and then the boars would have nothing to eat and a greater number would starve.)
- **Findings/Solutions:** What solutions might I consider if this problem continues? (Sample response: If the problem continues, a possible solution might be a mass eradication effort on the part of the hunters to wipe out the majority of the boar population.)
- **Modeling:** How might you model the different possibilities that could occur if humans intervened or if they didn't? (Students might create two tables where boars killed through human intervention increase or decrease.)
- **Perspectives/Audience:** What perspective are you considering as you think about this? What other perspectives need to be considered? (How might an animal activist examine this situation differently than a park ranger? How might a biologist and an ecologist examine this problem differently? Which

perspective is most relevant to the real problem? Who else might need to examine or be impacted by this problem?)

▪ **Processes/Methods:** What steps might you consider in finding out an answer to determine the impact the boars are having? (Sample response: First, study the effect on other producers and consumers. Second, look at the impact that the boar population growth is having on those organisms that consume the boars. Third, look at the number of acres of crops destroyed each year by the boars.)

▪ **Cause and Effect:** What are the effects that might occur if humans don't intervene? (Sample response: The boar population might grow large enough that they begin consuming crops that were meant for humans. Humans would have to get their food elsewhere or spend money to build new fences to keep boars out. The boar population could grow so large that the boars eat all of the producers and then the boars would begin to starve to death.)

▪ **Stability and Change:** Are the changes that are occurring as a result of the increase or decline of the wild boar population positive, negative, or neutral? (Sample response: The changes for boars are negative because they are leading to a decrease in the tuber population and they are destroying local crops.)

▪ **Systems/Energy and Matter:** How does this affect the consumption and flow of energy within the ecosystem? How might this affect other living systems, such as animals or plants? (Sample response: The increase in boar population influences the number of producers being consumed and the flow of energy into other living organisms.)

▪ **Scale and Proportion:** Is the boar population contained, or might it increase and spread in negative ways if humans don't intervene? (Sample response: The boar population could continue to increase and spread in negative ways, but only if the boars are able to find enough sources of food.)

▪ **Patterns:** What patterns do we notice about animal movement or deaths (based on graphs, models, or experiments that have been conducted)?

▪ **Structure and Function:** What function does the boar serve in the environment? What about the plants the boars are eating? (Sample response: The boar serves as a consumer within its environment. The boar droppings also help spread seeds and fertilize the soil. The tubers help keep the soil from eroding and provide energy for consumers.)

Step 3: Combine elements for complexity. Discuss how multiple elements interact to establish an overall interpretation of the problem.

▪ **Structure and Function + Systems/Energy and Matter:** How are the wild boar overpopulation and the flow of energy through the ecosystem related? (Sample response: The increase in the wild boar population means that the energy stored in the producers flows to more boars than other consumers. This disrupts the flow of energy, as not as much is available to other organisms that might consume the tubers.)

- **Cause and Effect + Perspectives/Audience:** How might an ecologist or biologist view the effects of the overpopulation of wild boars similarly or differently? (Sample response: Ecologists and biologists might see it as a natural cycle within the ecosystem and suggest that, in time, balance would be restored as the boar population grew to the point where, due to a lack of food sources, starvation set in and the population returned to normal.)

- **Findings/Solutions + Scale and Proportion:** What solutions have others tried, and have they reduced the environmental impact of the wild boars? What other solutions might work to reduce the overall impact of the wild boars on the plant life? (Sample response: Farmers have built fences around their crops and special traps to capture the boars. Hunters have increased the number of boars killed. For the most part this has not been effective enough to drastically reduce the population growth among wild boars.)

- **Scientific Information + Evidence/Data:** Who else has studied this, and how did their findings or solutions impact the questions you need to ask or answer? How might their evidence or data information the new questions you need to study? (Sample response: Scientists have looked at the increase in boar populations and their spread to other states. Millions of dollars have been spent on building new traps and increasing the number of people who are paid to hunt the boars. Radio collars have been attached to some boars, and scientists have used GPS to track their movement, hoping to understand migratory patterns so they can capture the boars in greater numbers.)

Appendix B

Blank Models and Guides

BLANK LITERARY ANALYSIS WHEEL—PRIMARY

Directions: Draw arrows across elements to show connections.

Text: _____

Feelings of Author (Tone)
and Reader (Mood)

Use of
Words/Techniques

Setting

Sequence/
Plot

Conflict/
Problem

Characters

Theme

Point of View

Structure and Style

Interpretation

Created by Tamra Stambaugh, Ph.D., & Emily Mofield, Ed.D., 2017.

LITERARY ANALYSIS WHEEL—PRIMARY GUIDE

Directions: Draw arrows across elements to show connections.

Text: _____

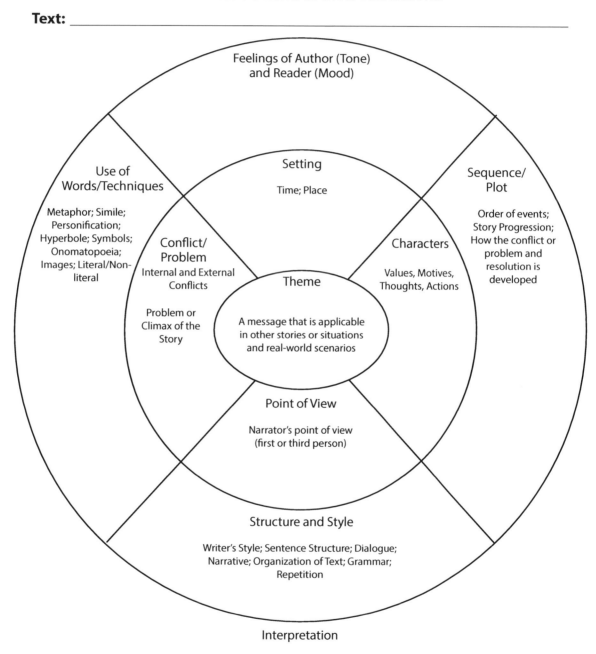

Feelings of Author (Tone)
and Reader (Mood)

Use of
Words/Techniques

Metaphor; Simile;
Personification;
Hyperbole; Symbols;
Onomatopoeia;
Images; Literal/Non-
literal

Setting

Time; Place

Sequence/
Plot

Order of events;
Story Progression;
How the conflict or
problem and
resolution is
developed

Conflict/
Problem

Internal and External
Conflicts

Problem or
Climax of the
Story

Theme

A message that is applicable
in other stories or situations
and real-world scenarios

Characters

Values, Motives,
Thoughts, Actions

Point of View

Narrator's point of view
(first or third person)

Structure and Style

Writer's Style; Sentence Structure; Dialogue;
Narrative; Organization of Text; Grammar;
Repetition

Interpretation

Created by Tamra Stambaugh, Ph.D., & Emily Mofield, Ed.D., 2017.

LITERARY ANALYSIS CUBES

Directions: Cut out each cube, fold along the lines, and glue or tape the tabs inside the cube.

Language/
Use of Words

Point of
View

Structure/
Style

Theme

Setting

Plot

Created by Tamra Stambaugh, Ph.D., & Emily Mofield, Ed.D., 2017.

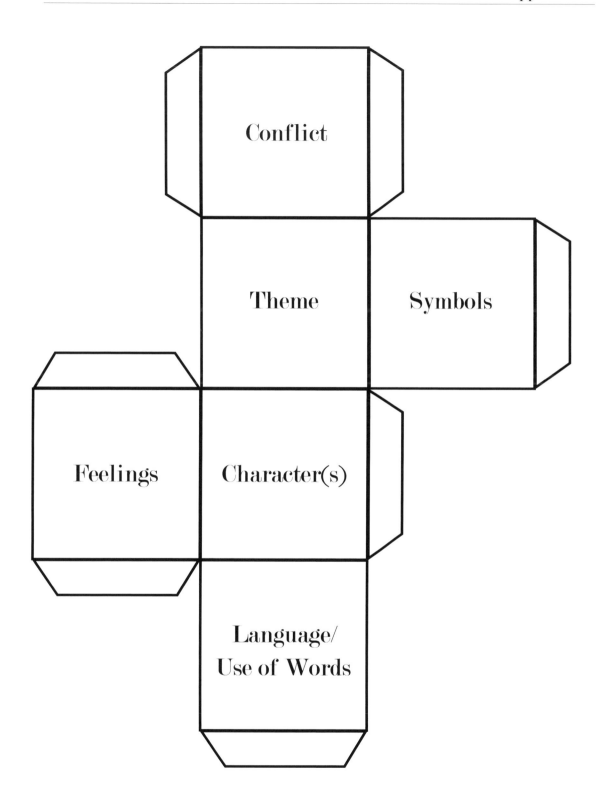

Conflict

Theme

Symbols

Feelings

Character(s)

Language/
Use of Words

Created by Tamra Stambaugh, Ph.D., & Emily Mofield, Ed.D., 2017.

BLANK VISUAL ANALYSIS WHEEL

Directions: Draw arrows across elements to show connections.

Art Piece: _____

Purpose/Context

Point of View

Images

Techniques

Emotions

Main Idea

Artist
Background

Structure/
Organization

Implications

Evaluation

Created by Tamra Stambaugh, Ph.D., & Emily Mofield, Ed.D., 2015.

VISUAL ANALYSIS WHEEL GUIDE

Directions: Draw arrows across elements to show connections.

Art Piece: _____

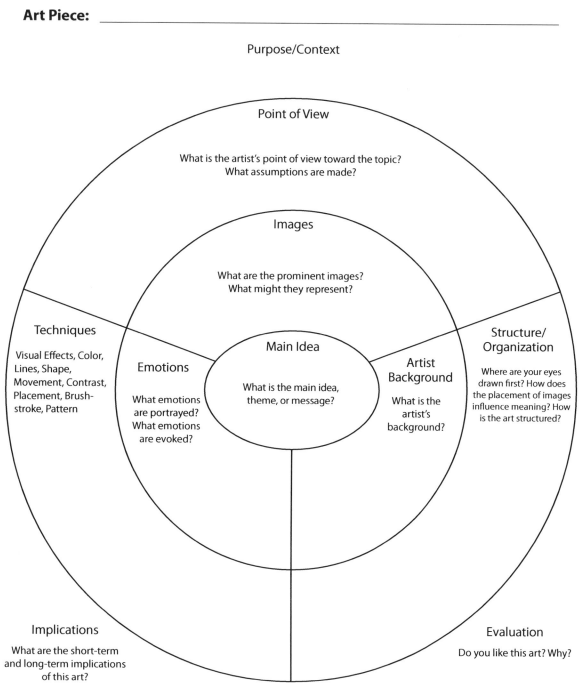

Purpose/Context

Point of View

What is the artist's point of view toward the topic?
What assumptions are made?

Images

What are the prominent images?
What might they represent?

Techniques

Visual Effects, Color,
Lines, Shape,
Movement, Contrast,
Placement, Brush-
stroke, Pattern

Emotions

What emotions
are portrayed?
What emotions
are evoked?

Main Idea

What is the main idea,
theme, or message?

Artist
Background

What is the
artist's
background?

Structure/
Organization

Where are your eyes
drawn first? How does
the placement of images
influence meaning? How
is the art structured?

Implications

What are the short-term
and long-term implications
of this art?

Evaluation

Do you like this art? Why?

Created by Tamra Stambaugh, Ph.D., & Emily Mofield, Ed.D., 2015.

VISUAL ANALYSIS CUBES

Directions: Cut out each cube, fold along the lines, and glue or tape the tabs inside the cube.

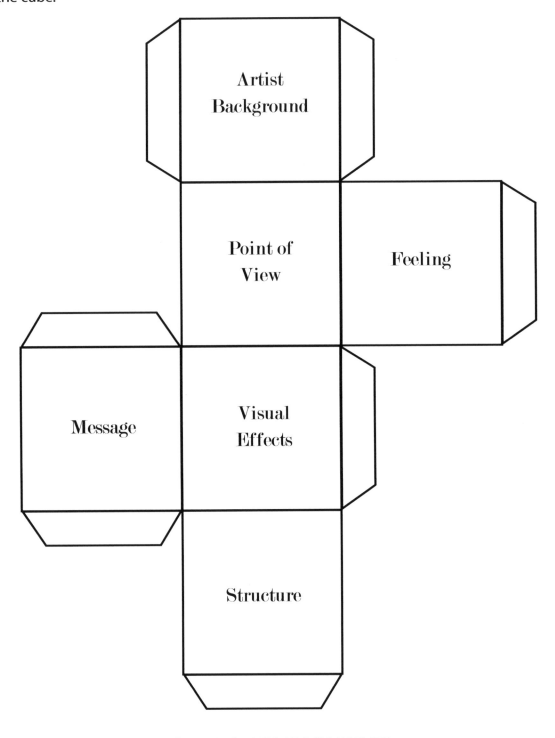

Artist Background

Point of View

Feeling

Message

Visual Effects

Structure

Created by Tamra Stambaugh, Ph.D., & Emily Mofield, Ed.D., 2017.

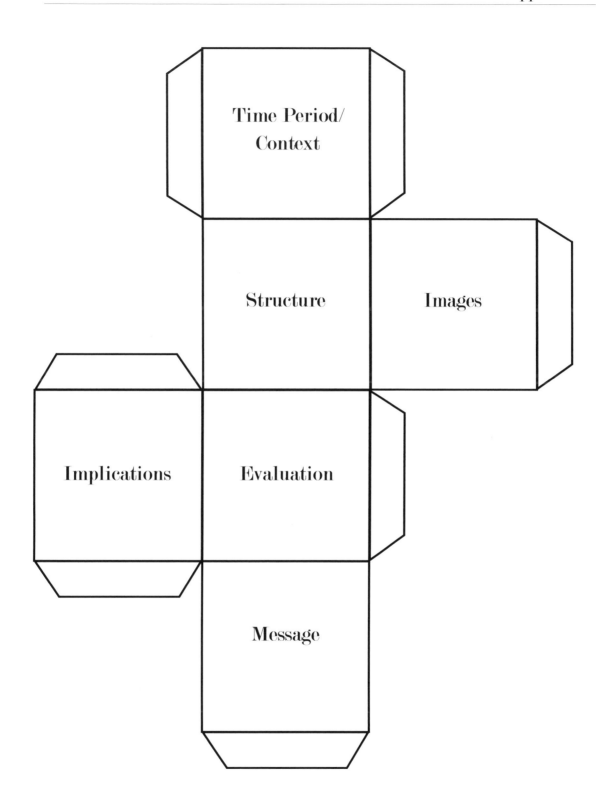

Time Period/
Context

Structure

Images

Implications

Evaluation

Message

Created by Tamra Stambaugh, Ph.D., & Emily Mofield, Ed.D., 2017.

BLANK TEXT ANALYSIS WHEEL—PRIMARY

Directions: Draw arrows across elements to show connections.

Text: _____

Point of View

Supporting Details

Techniques/
Structure

Supporting
Details

Main Idea or
Message

Supporting
Details

Context/Audience/
Purpose

Implications

Created by Tamra Stambaugh, Ph.D., & Emily Mofield, Ed.D., 2017.

TEXT ANALYSIS WHEEL—PRIMARY GUIDE

Directions: Draw arrows across elements to show connections.

Text: _____

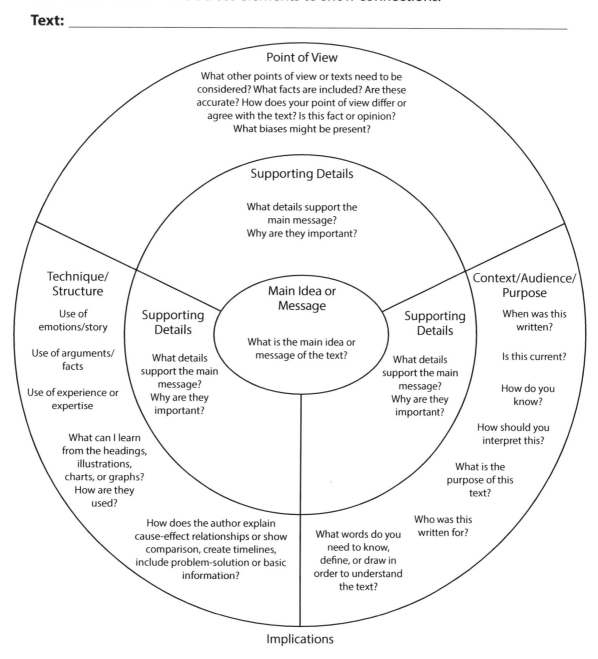

Point of View

What other points of view or texts need to be considered? What facts are included? Are these accurate? How does your point of view differ or agree with the text? Is this fact or opinion? What biases might be present?

Supporting Details

What details support the main message? Why are they important?

Technique/Structure

Use of emotions/story

Use of arguments/facts

Use of experience or expertise

What can I learn from the headings, illustrations, charts, or graphs? How are they used?

Supporting Details

What details support the main message? Why are they important?

Main Idea or Message

What is the main idea or message of the text?

Supporting Details

What details support the main message? Why are they important?

Context/Audience/Purpose

When was this written?

Is this current?

How do you know?

How should you interpret this?

What is the purpose of this text?

Who was this written for?

How does the author explain cause-effect relationships or show comparison, create timelines, include problem-solution or basic information?

What words do you need to know, define, or draw in order to understand the text?

Implications

Created by Tamra Stambaugh, Ph.D., & Emily Mofield, Ed.D., 2017.
Some questions are adapted from the CCSS for ELA (National Governors Association for Best Practices & Council of Chief State School Officers, 2010).

BLANK SCIENCE ANALYSIS WHEEL

Real-World Issue or Problem: _____

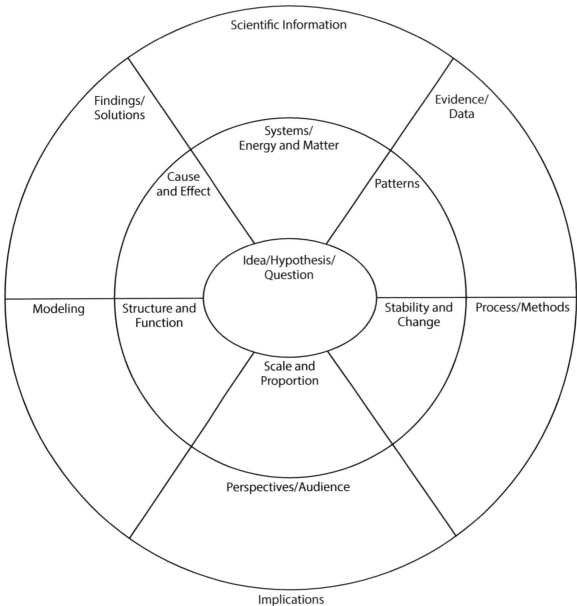

Created by Tamra Stambaugh, Ph.D., & Emily Mofield, Ed.D., 2017.
The middle section of the Science Analysis Wheel is adapted from the Next Generation Science Standards Crosscutting Concepts (National Research Council, 2012).

SCIENCE ANALYSIS WHEEL GUIDE

Real-World Issue or Problem: _____

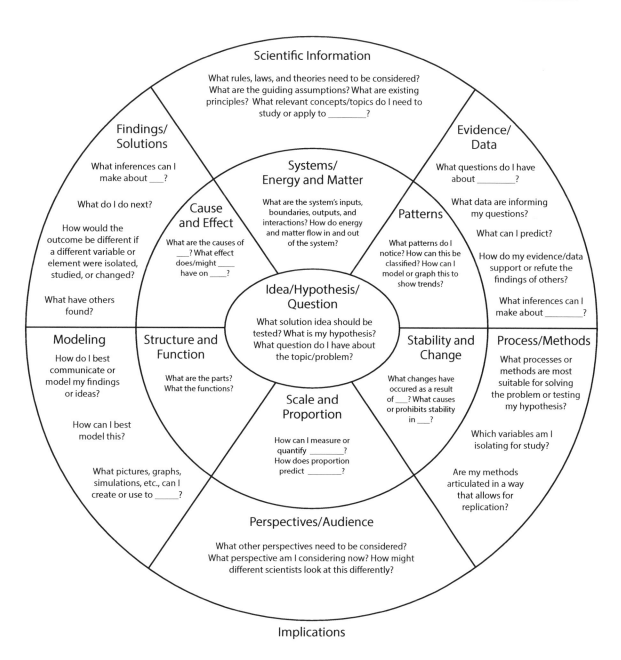

Created by Tamra Stambaugh, Ph.D., & Emily Mofield, Ed.D., 2017.
The middle section of the Science Analysis Wheel is adapted from the Next Generation Science Standards Crosscutting Concepts (National Research Council, 2012).

CONCEPT ORGANIZER

Directions: Which generalizations are most evident in this lesson, book, story, poem, or problem? Write the number of the generalization(s) and evidence you have. What new generalizations or connections can you make to other concepts?

1. Interactions are inevitable.
2. Interactions allow for changes.
3. Interactions are caused by multiple influences.
4. Interactions can be positive, negative, or mutually beneficial.

	Book, Story, Poem, Art, Problem: _____ _____	Book, Story, Poem, Art, Problem: _____ _____
Interaction Generalization(s) *(Write the Corresponding Number)*		
Explanation and Evidence for the Generalizations		
Connections to Other Ideas and Concepts		

Appendix C

Rubrics

RUBRIC 1: PRODUCT RUBRIC

Name: _____ Date: _____ Lesson: _____

	Unacceptable/ Needs Improvement	Fair	Acceptable	Excellent
Completion	Not turned in or late.	Missing key pieces.	Completed but lacks thought and professionalism.	Satisfactorily meets all requirements and expectations of the task.
Content/ Concept	Limited or vague connection.	Little connection from lesson content is made to interaction ideas.	Accurately relates lesson content ideas of interactions to assignment.	Insightfully relates the theme of interactions to assignment.
Thinking	Limited or vague evidence.	Reasoning is inaccurate, lacks originality, logical conclusions, or substantial claims.	Demonstrates some evidence of higher level thinking (creativity, evaluation, or analysis).	Demonstrates substantial evidence of higher level thinking (creativity, analysis, or evaluation with evidence).
Student-Developed Criteria				

Comments:

RUBRIC 2: CULMINATING PROJECT RUBRIC

Name: _____   Date: _____   Lesson: _____

	Unacceptable/ Needs Improvement	Fair	Acceptable	Excellent
Completion	Not turned in or late.	Missing key pieces	Completed but lacks thought and professionalism.	Satisfactorily meets all requirements and expectations of the task.
Evidence	Limited or no evidence.	Little support or elaboration to support ideas and generalizations.	Gives support/elaboration to support ideas.	Gives meaningful support/elaboration to support ideas and generalizations.
Concept	Limited or vague connection.	Little connection from unit content is made to the big idea of interactions.	Accurately relates ideas of interactions to assignment.	Insightfully relates the big idea of interactions to assignment.
Content	Limited or no content application.	Vague connections are made to content.	Some connections to content are made with some evidence.	Synthesizes content across lessons with substantial support and evidence.
Process	Limited or vague evidence.	Reasoning is inaccurate, lacks originality, logical conclusions, or substantial claims.	Demonstrates some evidence of higher level thinking (creativity, evaluation, or analysis).	Provides insightful evidence to support higher level thinking (creativity, evaluation, or analysis) in developing complex conclusions.
Student-Developed Criteria				

Comments:

About the Authors

Tamra Stambaugh, Ph.D., is an assistant research professor in special education and executive director of Programs for Talented Youth at Vanderbilt University. Stambaugh conducts research in gifted education with a focus on students living in rural settings, students of poverty, and curriculum and instructional interventions that promote gifted student learning. She is a frequent keynote speaker at national and international conferences and the coauthor/editor of several books and book chapters focused on curriculum and instructional development and differentiation, gifted students from low-income households, and gifted students from rural backgrounds.

Stambaugh is the recipient of several awards, including the Margaret The Lady Thatcher Medallion for scholarship, service, and character from the William & Mary School of Education; the Doctoral Student Award, Early Leader Award, and multiple curriculum awards from the National Association for Gifted Children; the Legacy Book Award for best scholarly new book in 2015 from the Texas Association for Gifted and Talented; the Jo Patterson Service Award and Curriculum Award from the Tennessee Association for Gifted Children; and the Higher Education Award from the Ohio Association for Gifted Children.

Eric Fecht, Ed.D., is an educational consultant for Vanderbilt Programs for Talented Youth. He supports a number of programs and special projects, including the Reading Academy at Vanderbilt. He taught elementary and middle school in Baltimore, MD, before helping develop gifted and talented programs in public schools in Abu Dhabi, U.A.E. He regularly consults with teachers who work with low-income gifted students and is involved in research related to serving low-income gifted students, relevancy in middle school literacy, and coaching teachers of gifted students.

Emily Mofield, Ed.D., is the lead consulting teacher for gifted education for Sumner County Schools in Tennessee and is involved in supporting several projects with Vanderbilt Programs for Talented Youth. She has also taught as a gifted education language arts middle school teacher for 10 years and currently serves as the NAGC Chair-Elect for Curriculum Studies. She regularly presents professional development on effective differentiation for advanced learners. She is a National Board Certified Teacher in language arts and has been recognized as the Tennessee Association for Gifted Children Teacher of the Year. She has received several NAGC Curriculum awards for the Vanderbilt PTY units coauthored with Tamra Stambaugh. She has also authored several research publications focused on social-emotional needs of gifted students and is the corecipient (with Megan Parker Peters) of the NAGC Hollingworth Award for her research on growth mindset, perfectionism, and underachievement.

Common Core State Standards for English Language Arts Alignment

Lesson	Accelerated CCSS for ELA
Lesson 1	RL.4.1 Refer to details and examples in a text when explaining what the text says explicitly and when drawing inferences from the text.
	RL.4.2 Determine a theme of a story, drama, or poem from details in the text; summarize the text.
	RL.4.3 Describe in depth a character, setting, or event in a story or drama, drawing on specific details in the text (e.g., a character's thoughts, words, or actions).
	RL.4.7 Make connections between the text of a story or drama and a visual or oral presentation of the text, identifying where each version reflects specific descriptions and directions in the text.
	RI.4.2 Determine the main idea of a text and explain how it is supported by key details; summarize the text.
	RI.4.6 Compare and contrast a firsthand and secondhand account of the same event or topic; describe the differences in focus and the information provided.
	W.4.2d Use precise language and domain-specific vocabulary to inform about or explain the topic.
	W.4.9 Draw evidence from literary or informational texts to support analysis, reflection, and research.
	SL.5.1c Pose and respond to specific questions by making comments that contribute to the discussion and elaborate on the remarks of others.
	SL.4.1d Review the key ideas expressed and draw conclusions in light of information and knowledge gained from the discussions.

Lesson	Accelerated CCSS for ELA
Lesson 1, *continued*	L.4.6 Acquire and use accurately grade-appropriate general academic and domain-specific words and phrases, including those that signal precise actions, emotions, or states of being (e.g., quizzed, whined, stammered) and that are basic to a particular topic (e.g., wildlife, conservation, and endangered when discussing animal preservation).
Lesson 2	W.4.2b Develop the topic with facts, definitions, concrete details, quotations, or other information and examples related to the topic.
	W.4.2d Use precise language and domain-specific vocabulary to inform about or explain the topic.
	L.4.6 Acquire and use accurately grade-appropriate general academic and domain-specific words and phrases, including those that signal precise actions, emotions, or states of being (e.g., quizzed, whined, stammered) and that are basic to a particular topic (e.g., wildlife, conservation, and endangered when discussing animal preservation).
Lesson 3	RL.4.2 Determine a theme of a story, drama, or poem from details in the text; summarize the text.
	RL.4.3 Describe in depth a character, setting, or event in a story or drama, drawing on specific details in the text (e.g., a character's thoughts, words, or actions).
	RL.5.1 Quote accurately from a text when explaining what the text says explicitly and when drawing inferences from the text.
	RL.5.3 Compare and contrast two or more characters, settings, or events in a story or drama, drawing on specific details in the text (e.g., how characters interact).
	RL.5.5 Explain how a series of chapters, scenes, or stanzas fits together to provide the overall structure of a particular story, drama, or poem.
	W.4.9 Draw evidence from literary or informational texts to support analysis, reflection, and research.
	SL.5.1a Come to discussions prepared, having read or studied required material; explicitly draw on that preparation and other information known about the topic to explore ideas under discussion.
	SL.5.1c Pose and respond to specific questions by making comments that contribute to the discussion and elaborate on the remarks of others.
	SL.5.1d Review the key ideas expressed and draw conclusions in light of information and knowledge gained from the discussions.

Lesson	Accelerated CCSS for ELA
Lesson 3, *continued*	L.4.6 Acquire and use accurately grade-appropriate general academic and domain-specific words and phrases, including those that signal precise actions, emotions, or states of being (e.g., quizzed, whined, stammered) and that are basic to a particular topic (e.g., wildlife, conservation, and endangered when discussing animal preservation).
Lesson 4	W.4.2d Use precise language and domain-specific vocabulary to inform about or explain the topic.
	W.4.3d Use concrete words and phrases and sensory details to convey experiences and events precisely.
	SL.5.1c Pose and respond to specific questions by making comments that contribute to the discussion and elaborate on the remarks of others.
	SL.5.1d Review the key ideas expressed and draw conclusions in light of information and knowledge gained from the discussions.
Lesson 5	W.4.2d Use precise language and domain-specific vocabulary to inform about or explain the topic.
	W.4.3d Use concrete words and phrases and sensory details to convey experiences and events precisely.
	SL.4.1d Review the key ideas expressed and draw conclusions in light of information and knowledge gained from the discussions.
	SL.5.2 Summarize a written text read aloud or information presented in diverse media and formats, including visually, quantitatively, and orally.
	L.4.6 Acquire and use accurately grade-appropriate general academic and domain-specific words and phrases, including those that signal precise actions, emotions, or states of being (e.g., quizzed, whined, stammered) and that are basic to a particular topic (e.g., wildlife, conservation, and endangered when discussing animal preservation).
Lesson 6	RL.4.1 Refer to details and examples in a text when explaining what the text says explicitly and when drawing inferences from the text.
	RL.4.3 Describe in depth a character, setting, or event in a story or drama, drawing on specific details in the text (e.g., a character's thoughts, words, or actions).
	RL.4.5 Explain major differences between poems, drama, and prose, and refer to the structural elements of poems (e.g., verse, rhythm, meter) and drama (e.g., casts of characters, settings, descriptions, dialogue, stage directions) when writing or speaking about a text.

Lesson	Accelerated CCSS for ELA
Lesson 6, *continued*	RL.5.2 Determine a theme of a story, drama, or poem from details in the text, including how characters in a story or drama respond to challenges or how the speaker in a poem reflects upon a topic; summarize the text.
	RL.5.5 Explain how a series of chapters, scenes, or stanzas fits together to provide the overall structure of a particular story, drama, or poem.
	RL.5.9 Compare and contrast stories in the same genre (e.g., mysteries and adventure stories) on their approaches to similar themes and topics.
	W.4.2d Use precise language and domain-specific vocabulary to inform about or explain the topic.
	W.4.3d Use concrete words and phrases and sensory details to convey experiences and events precisely.
	W.4.9 Draw evidence from literary or informational texts to support analysis, reflection, and research.
	SL.5.1a Come to discussions prepared, having read or studied required material; explicitly draw on that preparation and other information known about the topic to explore ideas under discussion.
Lesson 7	RI.4.7 Interpret information presented visually, orally, or quantitatively (e.g., in charts, graphs, diagrams, time lines, animations, or interactive elements on Web pages) and explain how the information contributes to an understanding of the text in which it appears.
	W.4.2b Develop the topic with facts, definitions, concrete details, quotations, or other information and examples related to the topic.
	W.4.2d Use precise language and domain-specific vocabulary to inform about or explain the topic.
	SL.5.1d Review the key ideas expressed and draw conclusions in light of information and knowledge gained from the discussions.
	L.4.6 Acquire and use accurately grade-appropriate general academic and domain-specific words and phrases, including those that signal precise actions, emotions, or states of being (e.g., quizzed, whined, stammered) and that are basic to a particular topic (e.g., wildlife, conservation, and endangered when discussing animal preservation).
Lesson 8	RL.4.1 Refer to details and examples in a text when explaining what the text says explicitly and when drawing inferences from the text.
	RL.4.2 Determine a theme of a story, drama, or poem from details in the text; summarize the text.

Lesson	Accelerated CCSS for ELA
Lesson 8, *continued*	RL.4.3 Describe in depth a character, setting, or event in a story or drama, drawing on specific details in the text (e.g., a character's thoughts, words, or actions).
	RL.4.6 Compare and contrast the point of view from which different stories are narrated, including the difference between first- and third-person narrations.
	RL.4.9 Compare and contrast the treatment of similar themes and topics (e.g., opposition of good and evil) and patterns of events (e.g., the quest) in stories, myths, and traditional literature from different cultures.
	RL.5.3 Compare and contrast two or more characters, settings, or events in a story or drama, drawing on specific details in the text (e.g., how characters interact).
Lesson 9	RL.4.1 Refer to details and examples in a text when explaining what the text says explicitly and when drawing inferences from the text.
	RL.4.2 Determine a theme of a story, drama, or poem from details in the text; summarize the text.
	RL.4.3 Describe in depth a character, setting, or event in a story or drama, drawing on specific details in the text (e.g., a character's thoughts, words, or actions).
	RL.4.7 Make connections between the text of a story or drama and a visual or oral presentation of the text, identifying where each version reflects specific descriptions and directions in the text.
	RL.5.3 Compare and contrast two or more characters, settings, or events in a story or drama, drawing on specific details in the text (e.g., how characters interact).
	RI.4.2 Determine the main idea of a text and explain how it is supported by key details; summarize the text.
	W.4.1b Provide reasons that are supported by facts and details.
	W.4.1c Link opinion and reasons using words and phrases (e.g., for instance, in order to, in addition).
	W.4.2d Use precise language and domain-specific vocabulary to inform about or explain the topic.
	SL.5.2 Summarize a written text read aloud or information presented in diverse media and formats, including visually, quantitatively, and orally.
	SL.5.3 Summarize the points a speaker makes and explain how each claim is supported by reasons and evidence.

Lesson	Accelerated CCSS for ELA
Lesson 10	W.4.2b Develop the topic with facts, definitions, concrete details, quotations, or other information and examples related to the topic.
	W.4.2d Use precise language and domain-specific vocabulary to inform about or explain the topic.
	W.4.3d Use concrete words and phrases and sensory details to convey experiences and events precisely.
	W.4.9 Draw evidence from literary or informational texts to support analysis, reflection, and research.
	L.4.6 Acquire and use accurately grade-appropriate general academic and domain-specific words and phrases, including those that signal precise actions, emotions, or states of being (e.g., quizzed, whined, stammered) and that are basic to a particular topic (e.g., wildlife, conservation, and endangered when discussing animal preservation).
Lesson 11	RL.4.1 Refer to details and examples in a text when explaining what the text says explicitly and when drawing inferences from the text.
	RI.4.1 Refer to details and examples in a text when explaining what the text says explicitly and when drawing inferences from the text.
	RI.4.9 Integrate information from two texts on the same topic in order to write or speak about the subject knowledgeably.
	RI.5.3 Explain the relationships or interactions between two or more individuals, events, ideas, or concepts in a historical, scientific, or technical text based on specific information in the text.
	RI.5.9 Integrate information from several texts on the same topic in order to write or speak about the subject knowledgeably.
	W.4.9 Draw evidence from literary or informational texts to support analysis, reflection, and research.

Next Generation Science Standards Alignment

Lesson	Accelerated NGSS
Lesson 1	3-LS4-4. Make a claim about the merit of a solution to a problem caused when the environment changes and the types of plants and animals that live there may change.
Lesson 2	5-PS3-1. Use models to describe that energy in animals' food (used for body repair, growth, motion, and to maintain body warmth) was once energy from the sun.
Lesson 2	5-LS2-1. Develop a model to describe the movement of matter among plants, animals, decomposers, and the environment.
Lesson 5	3-LS2-1. Construct an argument that some animals form groups that help members survive.
Lesson 7	3-LS4-3. Construct an argument with evidence that in a particular habitat some organisms can survive well, some survive less well, and some cannot survive at all.
Lesson 7	3-LS4-4. Make a claim about the merit of a solution to a problem caused when the environment changes and the types of plants and animals that live there may change.
Lesson 7	5-LS2-1. Develop a model to describe the movement of matter among plants, animals, decomposers, and the environment.
Lesson 9	3-LS3-2. Use evidence to support the explanation that traits can be influenced by the environment.
Lesson 10	3-LS2-1. Construct an argument that some animals form groups that help members survive.

247